JAMESTOWN EDUCATION

Timed Readings Plus
in Mathematics

BOOK 3

**15 Two-Part Lessons with Questions for
Building Reading Fluency and Comprehension**

D1592234

Glencoe

New York, New York   Columbus, Ohio   Chicago, Illinois   Peoria, Illinois   Woodland Hills, California

JAMESTOWN EDUCATION

 **Glencoe**

The **McGraw·Hill** Companies

ISBN: 0-07-872661-1

Send all queries to:
Glencoe/McGraw-Hill
8787 Orion Place
Columbus, OH 43240-4027

1 2 3 4 5 6 7 8 9 10 021 10 09 08 07 06 05 04

CONTENTS

You probably talk at an average rate of about 150 words a minute. If you are a reader of average ability, you read at a rate of about 250 words a minute. So your reading speed is nearly twice as fast as your speaking or listening speed. This example shows that reading is one of the fastest ways to get information.

The purpose of this book is to help you increase your reading rate and understand what you read. The 15 lessons in this book will also give you practice in reading mathematics-related articles and in preparing for tests in which you must read and understand nonfiction passages within a certain time limit.

Reading Faster and Better

Following are some strategies that you can use to read the articles in each lesson.

Previewing

Previewing before you read is a very important step. This helps you to get an idea of what a selection is about and to recall any previous knowledge you have about the subject. Here are the steps to follow when previewing.

Read the title. Titles are designed not only to announce the subject but also to make the reader think. Ask yourself questions such as What can I learn from the title? What thoughts does it bring to mind?

What do I already know about this subject?

Read the first sentence. If it is short, read the first two sentences. The opening sentence is the writer's opportunity to get your attention. Some writers announce what they hope to tell you in the selection. Some writers state their purpose for writing; others just try to get your attention.

Read the last sentence. If it is short, read the final two sentences. The closing sentence is the writer's last chance to get ideas across to you. Some writers repeat the main idea once more. Some writers draw a conclusion—this is what they have been leading up to. Other writers summarize their thoughts; they tie all the facts together.

Skim the entire selection. Glance through the selection quickly to see what other information you can pick up. Look for anything that will help you read fluently and with understanding. Are there names, dates, or numbers? If so, you may have to read more slowly.

Reading for Meaning

Here are some ways to make sure you are making sense of what you read.

Build your concentration. You cannot understand what you read if you are not concentrating. When you discover that your thoughts are straying, correct the situation right away. Avoid distractions and distracting situations. Keep in mind the information you learned from previewing. This will help focus your attention on the selection.

Read in thought groups. Try to see meaningful combinations of words—phrases, clauses, or sentences. If you look at only one word at a time (called word-by-word reading), both your comprehension and your reading speed suffer.

Ask yourself questions. To sustain the pace you have set for yourself and to maintain a high level of concentration and comprehension, ask yourself questions such as What does this mean? or How can I use this information? as you read.

Finding the Main Ideas

The paragraph is the basic unit of meaning. If you can quickly discover and understand the main idea of each paragraph, you will build your comprehension of the selection.

Find the topic sentence. The topic sentence, which contains the main idea, often is the first sentence of a paragraph. It is followed by sentences that support, develop, or explain the main idea. Sometimes a topic sentence comes at the end of a paragraph. When it does, the supporting details come first, building the base for the topic sentence. Some paragraphs do not have a topic sentence; all of the sentences combine to create a meaningful idea.

Understand paragraph structure. Every well-written paragraph has a purpose. The purpose may be to inform, define, explain, or illustrate. The purpose should always relate to the main idea and expand on it. As you read each paragraph, see how the body of the paragraph tells you more about the main idea.

Relate ideas as you read. As you read the selection, notice how the writer puts together ideas. As you discover the relationship between the ideas, the main ideas come through quickly and clearly.

Mastering Reading Comprehension

Reading fast is not useful if you don't remember or understand what you read. The two exercises in Part A provide a check on how well you have understood the article.

Recalling Facts

These multiple-choice questions provide a quick check to see how well you recall important information from the article. As you learn to apply the reading strategies described earlier, you should be able to answer these questions more successfully.

Understanding Ideas

These questions require you to think about the main ideas in the article. Some main ideas are stated in the article; others are not. To answer some of the questions, you need to draw conclusions about what you read.

The five exercises in Part B require multiple answers. These exercises provide practice in applying comprehension and critical thinking skills that you can use in all your reading.

Recognizing Words in Context

Always check to see whether the words around an unfamiliar word—its context—can give you a clue to the word's meaning. A word generally appears in a context related to its meaning.

Suppose, for example, that you are unsure of the meaning of the word *expired* in the following passage:

> Vera wanted to check out a book, but her library card had expired. She had to borrow my card, because she didn't have time to renew hers.

You could begin to figure out the meaning of *expired* by asking yourself a question such as, What could have happened to Vera's library card that would make her need to borrow someone else's card? You might realize that if Vera had to renew her card, its usefulness must have come to an end or run out. This would lead you to conclude that the word *expired* must mean "to come to an end" or "to run out." You would be right. The context suggested the meaning.

Context can also affect the meaning of a word you already know. The word *key*, for instance, has many meanings. There are musical keys, door keys, and keys to solving a mystery. The context in which the word *key* occurs will tell you which meaning is correct.

Sometimes a word is explained by the words that immediately follow it. The subject of a sentence and your knowledge about that subject might also help you determine the meaning of an unknown word. Try to decide the meaning of the word *revive* in the following sentence:

> Sunshine and water will revive those drooping plants.

The compound subject is *sunshine* and *water*. You know that plants need light and water to survive and that drooping plants are not healthy. You can figure out that *revive* means "to bring back to health."

Distinguishing Fact from Opinion

Every day you are called upon to sort out fact and opinion. Because much of what you read and hear contains both facts and opinions, you need to be able to tell the two apart.

Facts are statements that can be proved. The proof must be objective and verifiable. You must be able to check for yourself to confirm a fact.

Look at the following facts. Notice that they can be checked for accuracy and confirmed. Suggested sources for verification appear in parentheses.

- Abraham Lincoln was the 16th president of the United States. (Consult biographies, social studies books, encyclopedias, and similar sources.)

- Earth revolves around the Sun. (Research in encyclopedias or astronomy books; ask knowledgeable people.)

- Dogs walk on four legs. (See for yourself.)

Opinions are statements that cannot be proved. There is no objective evidence you can consult to check the truthfulness of an opinion. Unlike facts, opinions express personal beliefs or judgments. Opinions reveal how someone feels about a subject, not the facts about that subject. You might agree or disagree with someone's opinion, but you cannot prove it right or wrong.

Look at the following opinions. The reasons these statements are classified as opinions appear in parentheses.

- Abraham Lincoln was born to be a president. (You cannot prove this by referring to birth records. There is no evidence to support this belief.)

- Earth is the only planet in our solar system where intelligent life exists. (There is no proof of this. It may be proved true some day, but for now it is just an educated guess—not a fact.)

- The dog is a human's best friend. (This is not a fact; your best friend might not be a dog.)

As you read, be aware that facts and opinions are often mixed together. Both are useful to you as a reader. But to evaluate what you read and to read intelligently, you need to know the difference between the two.

Keeping Events in Order

Sequence, or chronological order, is the order of events in a story or an article or the order of steps in a process. Paying attention to the sequence of events or steps will help you follow what is happening, predict what might happen next, and make sense of a passage.

To make the sequence as clear as possible, writers often use signal words to help the reader get a more exact idea of when things happen. Following is a list of frequently used signal words and phrases:

until	first
next	then
before	after
finally	later
when	while
during	now
at the end	by the time
as soon as	in the beginning

Signal words and phrases are also useful when a writer chooses to relate details or events out of sequence. You need to pay careful attention to determine the correct chronological order.

Making Correct Inferences

Much of what you read *suggests* more than it *says*. Writers often do not state ideas directly in a text. They can't. Think of the time and space it would take to state every idea. And think of how boring that would be! Instead, writers leave it to you, the reader, to fill in the information they leave out—to make inferences. You do this by combining clues in the story or article with knowledge from your own experience.

You make many inferences every day. Suppose, for example, that you are visiting a friend's house for the first time. You see a bag of kitty litter. You infer (make an inference) that the family has a cat. Another day you overhear a conversation. You catch the names of two actors and the words *scene, dialogue,* and *directing.* You infer that the people are discussing a movie or play.

In these situations and others like them, you infer unstated information from what you observe or read. Readers must make inferences in order to understand text.

Be careful about the inferences you make. One set of facts may suggest several inferences. Some of these inferences could be faulty. A correct inference must be supported by evidence.

Remember that bag of kitty litter that caused you to infer that your friend has a cat? That could be a faulty inference. Perhaps your friend's family uses the kitty litter on their icy sidewalks to create traction. To be sure your inference is correct, you need more evidence.

Understanding Main Ideas

The main idea is the most important idea in a paragraph or passage—the idea that provides purpose and direction. The rest of the selection explains, develops, or supports the main idea. Without a main idea, there would be only a collection of unconnected thoughts.

In the following paragraph, the main idea is printed in italics. As you read, observe how the other sentences develop or explain the main idea.

Typhoon Chris hit with full fury today on the central coast of Japan. Heavy rain from the storm flooded the area. High waves carried many homes into the sea. People now fear that the heavy rains will cause mudslides in the central part of the country. The number of people killed by the storm may climb past the 200 mark by Saturday.

In this paragraph, the main idea statement appears first. It is followed by sentences that explain, support, or give details. Sometimes the main idea appears at the end of a paragraph. Writers often put the main idea at the end of a paragraph when their purpose is to persuade or convince. Readers may be more open to a new idea if the reasons for it are presented first.

As you read the following paragraph, think about the overall impact of the supporting ideas. Their purpose is to persuade the reader that the main idea in the last sentence should be accepted.

Last week there was a head-on collision at Huntington and Canton streets. Just a month ago a pedestrian was struck there. Fortunately, she was only slightly injured. In the past year, there have been more accidents there than at any other corner in the city. In fact, nearly 10 percent of all accidents in the city occur at the corner. This intersection is very dangerous, and a traffic signal should be installed there before a life is lost.

The details in the paragraph progress from least important to most important. They achieve their full effect in the main idea statement at the end.

In many cases, the main idea is not expressed in a single sentence. The reader is called upon to interpret all of the ideas expressed in the paragraph and to decide upon a main idea. Read the following paragraph.

> The American author Jack London was once a pupil at the Cole Grammar School in Oakland, California. Each morning the class sang a song. When the teacher noticed that Jack wouldn't sing, she sent him to the principal. He returned to class with a note. The note said that Jack could be excused from singing with the class if he would write an essay every morning.

In this paragraph, the reader has to interpret the individual ideas and to decide on a main idea. This main idea seems reasonable: Jack London's career as a writer began with a punishment in grammar school.

Understanding the concept of the main idea and knowing how to find it is important. Transferring that understanding to your reading and study is also important.

Working Through a Lesson

Part A

1. **Preview the article.** Locate the timed selection in Part A of the lesson that you are going to read. Wait for your teacher's signal to preview. You will have 20 seconds for previewing. Follow the previewing steps described on page 2.

2. **Read the article.** When your teacher gives you the signal, begin reading. Read carefully so that you will be able to answer questions about what you have read. When you finish reading, look at the board and note your reading time. Write this time at the bottom of the page on the line labeled Reading Time.

3. **Complete the exercises.** Answer the 10 questions that follow the article. There are 5 fact questions and 5 idea questions. Choose the best answer to each question and put an X in that box.

4. **Correct your work.** Use the Answer Key at the back of the book to check your answers. Circle any wrong answer and put an X in the box you should have marked. Record the number of correct answers on the appropriate line at the end of the lesson.

Part B

1. **Preview and read the passage.** Use the same techniques you

used to read Part A. Think about what you are reading.

2. **Complete the exercises.** Instructions are given for answering each category of question. There are 15 responses for you to record.

3. **Correct your work.** Use the Answer Key at the back of the book. Circle any wrong answer and write the correct letter or number next to it. Record the number of correct answers on the appropriate line at the end of the lesson.

Plotting Your Progress

1. **Find your reading rate.** Turn to the Reading Rate graph on page 76. Put an X at the point where the vertical line that represents the lesson intersects your reading time, shown along the left-hand side. The right-hand side of the graph will reveal your words-per-minute reading speed.

2. **Find your comprehension score.** Add your scores for Part A and Part B to determine your total number of correct answers. Turn to the Comprehension Score graph on page 77. Put an X at the point where the vertical line that represents your lesson intersects your total correct answers, shown along the left-hand side. The right-hand side of the graph will show the percentage of questions you answered correctly.

3. **Complete the Comprehension Skills Profile.** Turn to page 78. Record your incorrect answers for the Part B exercises. The five Part B skills are listed along the bottom. There are five columns of boxes, one column for each question. For every incorrect answer, put an X in a box for that skill.

To get the most benefit from these lessons, you need to take charge of your own progress in improving your reading speed and comprehension. Studying these graphs will help you to see whether your reading rate is increasing and to determine what skills you need to work on. Your teacher will also review the graphs to check your progress.

TO THE TEACHER

About the Series

Timed Readings Plus in Mathematics includes five books at reading levels 4–8, with one book at each level. Book One contains material at a fourth-grade reading level; Book Two at a fifth-grade level, and so on. The readability level is determined by the New Dale-Chall Readability Formula and is not to be confused with grade or age level of the student. The books are designed for use with students at middle school level and above.

The purposes of the series are as follows:

- to provide systematic, structured reading practice that helps students improve their reading rate and comprehension skills

- to give students practice in reading and understanding informational articles in the content area of mathematics

- to give students experience in reading various text types—informational, expository, narrative, and prescriptive

- to prepare students for taking standardized tests that include timed reading passages in various content areas

- to provide materials with a wide range of reading levels so that students can continue to practice and improve their reading rate and comprehension skills

Because the books are designed for use with students at designated reading levels rather than in a particular grade, the mathematics topics in this series are not correlated to any grade-level curriculum. Most standardized tests require students to read and comprehend mathematics passages. This series provides an opportunity for students to become familiar with the particular requirements of reading mathematics. For example, the vocabulary in a mathematics article is important. Students need to know certain words in order to understand the concepts and the information.

Each book in the series contains 15 two-part lessons. Part A focuses on improving reading rate. This section of the lesson consists of a 400-word timed informational article on a mathematics topic followed by two multiple-choice exercises. Recalling Facts includes five fact questions; Understanding Ideas includes five critical thinking questions.

Part B concentrates on building mastery in critical areas of comprehension. This section consists of a nontimed passage—the "plus" passage—followed by five exercises that address five major comprehension skills. The passage varies in length; its subject matter relates to the content of the timed selection.

Timed Reading and Comprehension

Timed reading is the best-known method of improving reading speed. There is no point in someone's reading at an accelerated speed if the person does not understand what she or he is reading. Nothing is more important than comprehension in reading. The main purpose of reading is to gain knowledge and insight, to understand the information that the writer and the text are communicating.

Few students will be able to read a passage once and answer all of the questions correctly. A score of 70 or 80 percent correct is normal. If the student gets 90 or 100 percent correct, he or she is either reading too slowly or the material is at too low a reading level. A comprehension or critical thinking score of less than 70 percent indicates a need for improvement.

One method of improving comprehension and critical thinking skills is for the student to go back and study each incorrect answer. First, the student should reread the question carefully. It is surprising how many students get the wrong answer simply because they have not read the question carefully. Then the student should look back in the passage to find the place where the question is answered, reread that part of the passage, and think about how to arrive at the correct answer. It is important to be able to recognize a correct answer when it is embedded in the text. Teacher guidance or class discussion will help the student find an answer.

Speed Versus Comprehension

It is not unusual for comprehension scores to decline as reading rate increases during the early weeks of timed readings. If this happens, students should attempt to level off their speed—but not lower it—and concentrate more on comprehension. Usually, if students maintain the higher speed and concentrate on comprehension, scores will gradually improve and within a week or two be back up to normal levels of 70 to 80 percent.

It is important to achieve a proper balance between speed and comprehension. An inefficient reader typically reads everything at one speed, usually slowly. Some poor readers, however, read rapidly but without satisfactory comprehension. The practice that this series provides enables students to increase their reading speed while maintaining normal levels of comprehension.

Getting Started

As a rule, the passages in a book designed to improve reading speed should be relatively easy. The student should not have much difficulty with the vocabulary or the subject matter. Don't worry about the passages being too easy; students should see how quickly and efficiently they can read a passage.

Begin by assigning students to a level. A student should start with a book that is one level below his or her current reading level. If a student's reading level is not known, a suitable starting point would be one or two levels below the student's present grade in school.

Introduce students to the contents and format of the book they are using. Examine the book to see how it is organized. Talk about the parts of each lesson. Discuss the purpose of timed reading and the use of the progress graphs at the back of the book.

Timing the Reading

One suggestion for timing the reading is to have all students begin reading the selection at the same time. After one minute, write on the board the time that has elapsed and begin updating it at 10-second intervals (1:00, 1:10, 1:20, etc.). Another option is to have individual students time themselves with a stopwatch.

Teaching a Lesson

Part A

1. Give students the signal to begin previewing the lesson. Allow 20 seconds, and then discuss special terms or vocabulary that students found.

2. Use one of the methods previously described to time students as they read the passage. (Include the 20-second preview time as part of the first minute.) Tell students to write down the last time shown on the board or the stopwatch when they finish reading. Have them record the time in the designated space after the passage.

3. Next, have students complete the exercises in Part A. Work with them to check their answers, using the Answer Key that begins on page 74. Have them circle incorrect answers, mark the correct answers, and then record the number of correct answers for Part A on the appropriate line at the end of the lesson. Correct responses to eight or more questions indicate satisfactory comprehension and recall.

Part B

1. Have students read the Part B passage and complete the exercises that follow it. Directions are provided with each exercise. Correct responses require deliberation and discrimination.

2. Work with students to check their answers. Then discuss the answers with them and have them record the number of correct answers for Part B at the end of the lesson.

Have students study the correct answers to the questions they answered incorrectly. It is important that they understand why a particular answer is correct or incorrect. Have them reread relevant parts of a passage to clarify an answer. An effective cooperative activity is to have students work in pairs to discuss their answers, explain why they chose the answers they did, and try to resolve differences.

Monitoring Progress

Have students find their total correct answers for the lesson and record their reading time and scores on the graphs on pages 76 and 77. Then have them complete the Comprehension Skills Profile on page 78. For each incorrect response to a question in Part B, students should mark an X in the box above each question type.

The legend on the Reading Rate graph automatically converts reading times to words-per-minute rates. The Comprehension Score graph automatically converts the raw scores to percentages.

These graphs provide a visual record of a student's progress. This record gives the student and you an opportunity to evaluate the student's progress and to determine the types of exercises and skills he or she needs to concentrate on.

Diagnosis and Evaluation

The following are typical reading rates.

Slow Reader—150 Words Per Minute

Average Reader—250 Words Per Minute

Fast Reader—350 Words Per Minute

A student who consistently reads at an average or above-average rate (with satisfactory comprehension) is ready to advance to the next book in the series.

A column of X's in the Comprehension Skills Profile indicates a specific comprehension weakness. Using the profile, you can assess trends in student performance and suggest remedial work if necessary.

Geometry is the study of points, lines, curves, and surfaces. We use our knowledge of geometry to describe locations on Earth.

Have you ever noticed the lines on a globe? The horizontal lines that circle the earth are called lines of latitude. These imaginary lines are also known as parallels. This is because they are straight and always the same distance apart from each other. The equator is the parallel line that divides the earth into two equal parts. It is the longest line of latitude. *Latitude* comes from the Latin word *latus*, meaning "wide." It measures distance in degrees north or south of the equator, which is at 0 degrees latitude.

The vertical lines on a globe that go through the North and South Poles are called lines of longitude, or meridians. *Longitude* comes from the Latin word *longus*, meaning "length." It measures distance in degrees east or west of the prime meridian, which is 0 degrees longitude. The prime meridian is an imaginary line that passes through Greenwich, England.

Geographers also divide the earth into hemispheres. Everything north of the equator is in the Northern Hemisphere, while everything south of the equator is in the Southern Hemisphere. The Western Hemisphere is west of the prime meridian, and the Eastern Hemisphere is east of the prime meridian.

On the opposite side of the earth from Greenwich, the Western and Eastern Hemispheres meet at the International Date Line. When it is noon along the prime meridian, it is midnight along the International Date Line. From the prime meridian, you can travel west halfway around the earth to the 180 degrees west longitude line. At the 180 degrees line, East meets West: 180 degrees east and 180 degrees west are the same line.

The earth, as represented on globes and maps, is divided into 360 degrees. Each degree is divided into 60 minutes, and each minute is divided into 60 seconds. Locations on the earth are made up of a crisscross of latitudes and longitudes. Each location tells you how far to go north or south from the equator and how far to go west or east from the prime meridian. The location of New York City is 40 degrees latitude (north of the equator), and 74 degrees longitude (west of Greenwich). Using minutes and seconds as well as degrees, the location of New York would be 40 degrees, 42 minutes, 51 seconds north; 74 degrees, 0 minutes, 23 seconds west.

Reading Time _____

Recalling Facts

1. Lines of latitude
   - ❑ a. measure distance east or west.
   - ❑ b. are also called parallels.
   - ❑ c. are also called meridians.

2. Longitude
   - ❑ a. runs parallel to latitude.
   - ❑ b. comes from the Latin word for length.
   - ❑ c. measures distance north and south.

3. The line at 0 degrees longitude is called the
   - ❑ a. equator.
   - ❑ b. International Date Line.
   - ❑ c. prime meridian.

4. Geographers divide the earth into
   - ❑ a. degrees.
   - ❑ b. coordinates.
   - ❑ c. hemispheres.

5. The _____ is an imaginary line that passes through Greenwich, England.
   - ❑ a. the equator.
   - ❑ b. the prime meridian.
   - ❑ c. the International Meridian Conference.

Understanding Ideas

6. One can conclude from this passage that one could leave Greenwich and reach the International Date Line by traveling
   - ❑ a. north.
   - ❑ b. east or west.
   - ❑ c. north or south.

7. Knowing that the earth is a circle and has 360 degrees tells you that halfway around it is
   - ❑ a. 180 degrees.
   - ❑ b. 90 degrees.
   - ❑ c. 270 degrees.

8. The equator is at 0 degrees latitude, so the South Pole is at
   - ❑ a. 180 degrees.
   - ❑ b. 90 degrees.
   - ❑ c. 270 degrees.

9. If it is 2:00 P.M. at the prime meridian, at the International Date Line it is
   - ❑ a. 10:00 A.M.
   - ❑ b. 4:00 P.M.
   - ❑ c. 2:00 A.M.

10. Which of the following statements is *not* true?
    - ❑ a. If you traveled from the prime meridian west halfway around the earth, you would reach 180 degrees west longitude.
    - ❑ b. If you traveled from the prime meridian east halfway around the earth, you would reach 180 degrees east longitude.
    - ❑ c. If you traveled from the South Pole north 180 degrees, you would reach the equator at 0 degrees latitude.

Finding Position Using the Sextant and Chronometer

In 1757 sailors began using the sextant to find their location at sea. A sextant is a triangular frame with one curved side. It is a handheld instrument with a telescope and two mirrors—one fixed, the other movable. Sailors looked through the telescope at the horizon. Next they adjusted the movable mirror until the image of the sun in the fixed mirror lined up with the horizon. They then read the angle of the movable mirror against a scale on the frame marked from 0 to 120 degrees. This angle is the elevation (height) of the sun above the horizon.

The sun reaches its greatest elevation at noon. At the equator, the sun is directly overhead. At the poles, it is close to the horizon. So measuring this elevation at noon told the sailor how far north or south of the equator he was—his latitude.

Finding longitude was more difficult. In the late 18th century sailors began to use a clock called a chronometer. The clock was set to the time at Greenwich, England (0 degrees longitude). Each hour of difference between, for example, local noontime and Greenwich's noontime equals 15 degrees of longitude. So a sailor who was 2.5 hours behind Greenwich time knew he was 37.5 degrees west of it.

1. **Recognizing Words in Context**

   Find the word *adjusted* in the passage. One definition below is closest to the meaning of that word. One definition has the opposite or nearly the opposite meaning. The remaining definition has a completely different meaning. Label the definitions C for *closest*, O for *opposite or nearly opposite*, and D for *different*.

   _____ a. folded

   _____ b. changed

   _____ c. kept steady

2. **Distinguishing Fact from Opinion**

   Two of the statements below present *facts*, which can be proved. The other statement is an *opinion*, which expresses someone's thoughts or beliefs. Label the statements F for *fact* and O for *opinion*.

   _____ a. Sailors first used the sextant in 1757.

   _____ b. A sextant helps sailors determine their latitude.

   _____ c. Navigating with a sextant is easy.

3. Keeping Events in Order

Number the statements below 1, 2, and 3 to show the order in which the steps take place.

_____ a. Look through the telescope and line up the sun with the horizon.

_____ b. Read the degree of elevation from the scale.

_____ c. Look for the sun in the sky.

4. Making Correct Inferences

Two of the statements below are correct *inferences*, or reasonable guesses. They are based on information in the passage. The other statement is an incorrect, or faulty, inference. Label the statements C for *correct* inference and F for *faulty* inference.

_____ a. The chronometer was used only to find longitude.

_____ b. It would be difficult to use a sextant on a rainy day.

_____ c. The sextant still is the most accurate measure of latitude used by sailors.

5. Understanding Main Ideas

One of the statements below expresses the main idea of the passage. One statement is too general, or too broad. The other explains only part of the passage; it is too narrow. Label the statements M for *main idea*, B for *too broad*, and N for *too narrow*.

_____ a. The sextant was used to measure the angle of the sun above the horizon.

_____ b. The sextant and the chronometer were useful tools for determining position at sea.

_____ c. Sailors used special instruments such as the sextant and the chronometer.

Correct Answers, Part A _____

Correct Answers, Part B _____

Total Correct Answers _____

Successful farming depends on careful study of costs to find out whether the farm would be able to make a profit. Costs include labor, tools and machines, fuel, plant materials, and fertilizer. Suppose a healthy Christmas tree farm can start to make money in as little as six years. Let's use some math to break these costs down and consider how much money a farm could expect to make.

First you must prepare your fields. You may need to use a heavy machine like a bulldozer to remove rocks or tree stumps. Next you need to plant and care for the new seedlings, or baby trees. Seedling prices will vary depending on where you live and who supplies the trees. For example, Fraser fir seedlings from a private tree nursery may cost $750 per 1,000. White pine seedlings from a state tree nursery might be less than $100 per 1,000. Planting and replacing dead seedlings could cost an extra $80 to $180 per acre.

Other costs include fencing to protect the trees against deer, weed control, and insect spray. All trees must be shaped by careful shearing to have a traditional Christmas tree shape. Shearing is done once during the growing season. For young trees, shearing can cost as low as $30 per acre. Costs may increase 10 times, however, before the trees are harvested.

The two most common ways to sell trees are choose-and-cut and retail. Choose-and-cut farms mark trees for harvest, and customers are free to wander about and select trees for cutting. Farmers will provide hand saws for people to cut their own trees, or they will cut down trees and move them out of the field for customers. Retail lots are neighborhood locations such as discount stores, gas stations, and farmers' markets. Choose-and-cut prices are about $10 to $25 per tree. On a retail lot, the same trees may sell for $25 to $40 per tree.

After considering the costs, let's say you buy 1,000 white pine seedlings from a state nursery for $100. You plant 1,000 on one acre of land. Your cost for everything else is $1,000 per acre per year. After six years, you will have invested $6,100 in your trees ($1,000 × 6 + $100). You sell your trees for an average price of $20. If you sell all 1,000 trees, your sales will be $20,000. Your gross profit is $13,900 per acre.

Reading Time _____

Recalling Facts

1. A Christmas tree farm can start to make money
   - ❏ a. in December.
   - ❏ b. in about six years.
   - ❏ c. in the first year.

2. Tree seedling prices depend upon
   - ❏ a. the type you buy.
   - ❏ b. the size of the seedlings.
   - ❏ c. where you buy them.

3. If you are planting trees in rough, rocky soil, you will probably need
   - ❏ a. more equipment for spraying.
   - ❏ b. a bulldozer.
   - ❏ c. to choose a new location.

4. Baby trees are called
   - ❏ a. white pines.
   - ❏ b. harvests.
   - ❏ c. seedlings.

5. Someone who wants a Christmas tree for the least money should
   - ❏ a. buy it retail at a discount store.
   - ❏ b. go to a place where customers cut their own trees.
   - ❏ c. grow one.

Understanding Ideas

6. One might infer from this passage that
   - ❏ a. starting a Christmas tree farm takes only some planning.
   - ❏ b. Christmas tree farming is a year-round job.
   - ❏ c. Christmas trees require less care than other tree crops.

7. One can conclude that farmers must shear the growing trees because
   - ❏ a. trees do not naturally grow into "Christmas tree" shape.
   - ❏ b. shearing helps the trees to grow in a healthy way.
   - ❏ c. shearing keeps the trees free from disease.

8. One can conclude that a Christmas tree farm
   - ❏ a. can be a profitable business.
   - ❏ b. is a very simple business.
   - ❏ c. requires especially rich land.

9. From the information in this passage, one can assume that
   - ❏ a. a farmer would pay much more to buy the trees than he would to take care of them.
   - ❏ b. what a farmer would pay for trees is greater than the profit he receives from them.
   - ❏ c. a farmer would pay much less to buy the trees than he would to take care of them.

10. One would infer from this passage that gross profit is
   - ❏ a. the difference between the money earned on your trees and the cost of growing them.
   - ❏ b. the retail price minus the cost of caring for the trees.
   - ❏ c. the highest price at which you can sell your trees.

Math for Growing Corn

Nature has the most control over how much corn is grown and how good it tastes. But certain farming practices can enhance results. Farmers know that corn should be planted early; spaced evenly; and protected from weeds, diseases, and insects. But weeds and insects, like plants, depend on temperature to grow. Farmers need to know when to start using pest control based on temperatures, rather than on the calendar.

Farmers often use the Growing Degree Days (GDD) system to calculate the average daily temperatures. A high GDD means warm growing days. The GDD will become lower as the fall season sets in and the growing days grow shorter.

GDD is computed as the average daily temperature minus 50. The GDD calculation normally uses the "86/50 cutoff method." If the actual daily temperature is greater than 86 degrees or less than 50 degrees Fahrenheit, 86 and 50 degrees are still used in the calculation.

For example, one day the high temperature is 90 degrees and the low temperature is 54 degrees. The GDD is calculated by adding the high and low temperatures and then dividing by 2 for the average (86 + 54 = 140, 140 ÷ 2 = 70). Then subtract 50. The GDD is 20.

1. Recognizing Words in Context

Find the word *enhance* in the passage. One definition below is closest to the meaning of that word. One definition has the opposite or nearly the opposite meaning. The remaining definition has a completely different meaning. Label the definitions C for *closest*, O for *opposite or nearly opposite*, and D for *different*.

_____ a. show clearly

_____ b. improve

_____ c. hold back

2. Distinguishing Fact from Opinion

Two of the statements below present *facts*, which can be proved. The other statement is an *opinion*, which expresses someone's thoughts or beliefs. Label the statements F for *fact* and O for *opinion*.

_____ a. Good farming practices can produce better crops.

_____ b. Farmers who don't use GDD would rather just use their own methods.

_____ c. The 86/50 cutoff method is used to calculate the GDD.

3. Keeping Events in Order

Number the statements below 1, 2, and 3 to show the order in which the steps should be performed.

_____ a. Calculate GDD by adding the high and low temperatures.

_____ b. Divide by 2 for the average.

_____ c. Subtract 50.

4. Making Correct Inferences

Two of the statements below are correct *inferences,* or reasonable guesses. They are based on information in the passage. The other statement is an incorrect, or faulty, inference. Label the statements C for *correct* inference and F for *faulty* inference.

_____ a. The GDD calculates temperature, not the number of days that corn is growing.

_____ b. A steady rise in GDD means that the weather is growing warmer.

_____ c. The GDD will tell a farmer how good the crop will be.

5. Understanding Main Ideas

One of the statements below expresses the main idea of the passage. One statement is too general, or too broad. The other explains only part of the passage; it is too narrow. Label the statements M for *main idea*, B for *too broad*, and N for *too narrow*.

_____ a. Math and science are important in farming.

_____ b. Farmers often use the GDD system to calculate the average daily temperatures.

_____ c. Many farmers who grow corn use GDD to calculate the best time to apply pest controls.

Correct Answers, Part A _____

Correct Answers, Part B _____

Total Correct Answers _____

3 A   Math in the Kitchen: How to Scale a Recipe Up or Down

How do cooks use recipes written for a certain number of people when they are cooking for more or fewer people? For example, a recipe for meatloaf may say that it serves four people. If you want to feed eight, you could make two separate meatloaves according to your recipe. But you could also multiply each of the ingredient amounts by two to double the overall amount of meatloaf. If you plan to serve only two, you could divide each of the ingredient amounts by two to halve the overall amount of meatloaf.

For best results, you should not scale a recipe up or down by a factor greater than four. If a recipe serves eight, the highest you should raise it to is 32 servings. The lowest you should decrease it to is two servings.

There is an even more accurate method for increasing or decreasing a recipe to suit your needs. It's done by finding the conversion factor between the original recipe and the amount you want and then multiplying each ingredient by that number.

Let's look at cases that are not as easy as scaling up or down by a factor of two. To calculate your conversion factor, divide the recipe's "old" yield into the "new" yield you want. For example, if you need only 8 ounces of sauce and your recipe yields 32 ounces, simply divide 8 (new) by 32 (old). Your conversion factor is 0.25 ($8 \div 32 = 0.25$).

You might want to make more than what the recipe yields. If you need 20 ounces of sauce and the recipe you have yields 8 ounces, divide 20 (new) by 8 (old). This gives a conversion factor of 2.5.

Now multiply each ingredient in the original recipe by the conversion factor. If the conversion factor is less than one, you're decreasing the recipe. If it's greater than one, you're increasing the recipe.

What about pan size? If the recipe calls for a 15-inch $\times$ 10-inch jelly roll pan and you've halved the recipe, you need half the pan area. Multiply the length of the pan by the width of the pan to get the square inches (15 inches $\times$ 10 inches = 150 square inches). Half of that is 75 square inches. An 11-inch $\times$ 7-inch rectangle pan equals 77 square inches.

But don't assume cooking times and temperatures are adjusted in the same way as ingredients or pan area. Doubling a recipe usually increases the baking time. You would need to watch your dish as it cooks.

Reading Time _____

Recalling Facts

1. To *halve* a recipe means
   - ❏ a. to multiply it by two.
   - ❏ b. to cook it to serve two people.
   - ❏ c. to divide it by two.

2. If a recipe serves eight, the most you should increase it to is
   - ❏ a. 16 servings.
   - ❏ b. 32 servings.
   - ❏ c. 2 servings.

3. To find the conversion factor for increasing or decreasing a recipe, you
   - ❏ a. divide the yield of the original recipe by the yield you want.
   - ❏ b. multiply the yield of the original recipe by the yield you want.
   - ❏ c. divide the yield you want by the yield of the original recipe.

4. To find the area of a cooking pan, you would _____ the width of the pan by the length of the pan.
   - ❏ a. subtract
   - ❏ b. divide
   - ❏ c. multiply

5. If the conversion factor is less than one, you are
   - ❏ a. decreasing the recipe.
   - ❏ b. increasing the recipe.
   - ❏ c. not changing the recipe.

Understanding Ideas

6. If your conversion factor is 2 and your original recipe calls for 1 tablespoon of lemon juice, you should use
   - ❏ a. 2 tablespoons of lemon juice.
   - ❏ b. 0.2 tablespoons of lemon juice.
   - ❏ c. 1 tablespoon of lemon juice.

7. If you have doubled a recipe that calls for an 8-inch $\times$ 8-inch cake pan, you would first multiply 8×8, then
   - ❏ a. multiply the product by 2.
   - ❏ b. divide the product by 2.
   - ❏ c. subtract the product by 2.

8. If you have increased a recipe that serves 12 by a factor of 1.5, you calculate
   - ❏ a. $12 + 1.5$.
   - ❏ b. $12 \div 1.5$.
   - ❏ c. 12×1.5.

9. If you need 32 ounces of sauce and your original recipe yields 8 ounces, you would
   - ❏ a. divide 8 by 32.
   - ❏ b. find the conversion factor and then multiply each ingredient by that number.
   - ❏ c. use a conversion factor of 2.

10. From this article, you could conclude that
    - ❏ a. using simple math, most recipes can be decreased or increased by any factor.
    - ❏ b. doubling and halving recipes can be done easily.
    - ❏ c. it's easier to increase a recipe than to decrease a recipe.

3   B   Cooking Around the World: Metric Measurements

You have promised to send your favorite cake recipe to your friend in Ireland. But recipes there use metric measurements. That's like another language for cooking. You want to make sure the cake will come out all right. So you need to change the measurements from U.S. standard to metric. It's not hard to do. You can do it with a conversion chart and a little math.

One important thing to know is that U.S. recipes measure all ingredients by volume (tablespoons, cups). But in other countries, it is common to measure only liquid ingredients by volume (milliliters, liters) and dry ingredients by weight (grams, kilograms).

Another thing to know is that recipes written in metric often do not use fractions. Let's say your recipe calls for a ⅓ cup of brown sugar (measured by volume, with fraction). The equal amount in metric would be 65 grams (measured by weight, without fractions). But you have to change ⅓ cup to the correct measurement in liters. The chart shows that 1 cup is equal to 0.24 liter. Change ⅓ to its decimal 0.33. Then multiply 0.33 by 0.24. You will need 0.08 liter of brown sugar to make your recipe. The rest should be a "piece of cake."

1. Recognizing Words in Context

Find the word *convert* in the passage. One definition below is closest to the meaning of that word. One definition has the opposite or nearly the opposite meaning. The remaining definition has a completely different meaning. Label the definitions C for *closest*, O for *opposite or nearly opposite*, and D for *different*.

_____ a. change from one form to another

_____ b. leave in its original form

_____ c. mix together

2. Distinguishing Fact from Opinion

Two of the statements below present *facts*, which can be proved. The other statement is an *opinion*, which expresses someone's thoughts or beliefs. Label the statements F for *fact* and O for *opinion*.

_____ a. The metric system has different measures for volume and weight.

_____ b. You can cook using a recipe written with either U.S. or metric standards.

_____ c. The United States should use the metric system.

3. Keeping Events in Order

Number the statements below 1, 2, and 3 to show the order in which the information was given in the passage.

_____ a. Multiply 0.33 by 0.24.

_____ b. Change the fraction ⅓ to a decimal to get 0.33.

_____ c. Convert 1 cup to 0.24 liter.

4. Making Correct Inferences

Two of the statements below are correct *inferences,* or reasonable guesses. They are based on information in the passage. The other statement is an incorrect, or faulty, inference. Label the statements C for *correct* inference and F for *faulty* inference.

_____ a. Metric measurements can be converted to U.S. standard measurements.

_____ b. Metric measurements are always stated in whole numbers.

_____ c. A recipe could be ruined if the measurements are not converted correctly.

5. Understanding Main Ideas

One of the statements below expresses the main idea of the passage. One statement is too general, or too broad. The other explains only part of the passage; it is too narrow. Label the statements M for *main idea,* B for *too broad,* and N for *too narrow.*

_____ a. U.S. recipes use a different measurement system than other countries use.

_____ b. Metric recipes measure liquid ingredients by volume and dry ingredients by weight.

_____ c. Recipes that use an unknown measurement system can be converted to a known system.

Correct Answers, Part A _____

Correct Answers, Part B _____

Total Correct Answers _____

The Math of Human Resources

How do companies decide whom to hire for a job? How much should the job pay? In large companies, decisions like these are made with help from the human resources (HR) department and mathematical formulas. First the job is described by making a complete list of all its duties. This job description is used to work out a scale grade for the job. Every grade is given a value based on the importance of the job to the overall success of the company. As the president of the company is thought to have the most valuable job, that job is ranked highest. Other jobs add lower levels of value to the company, and so are ranked with lower grades.

The HR department investigates what other companies in the same business pay for the same job grades. Then HR decides on salary ranges and midpoint salaries for job grades. For example, perhaps one range is from $20,000 to $40,000 a year. The midpoint, or mean, would be $30,000. Using this example, let's say someone with little experience is being hired for a job in a factory. This person's salary might be $20,000 a year, at the low end of the scale. Someone who has more experience and who might do the same job better would be offered a salary around the midpoint or the higher end of the scale. This is one way HR uses mathematics to decide how much to pay an employee.

Another important question for HR about any job is how much it costs the company to have a person work at that job. To answer this question, HR people can use a cost-of-employee calculator. The first figure in this calculation is the salary of the employee. Then if the employee receives a cash bonus or other extra money, those figures are also included. The next step is to collect information on benefits paid by the employer by asking these questions: How many paid vacation days a year will the employee receive? How many paid sick days a year does the employee get? Costs of taxes paid by the employer are figured next, followed by the costs of training the person for the job. The final step figures in all other expenses, such as tools or supplies used by the employee. In the end, the cost-of-employee calculator gives HR information such as the total cost of an employee to the company and, therefore, what should be the cost of an employee's hour of work.

Reading Time _____

Recalling Facts

1. HR departments use mathematical formulas to
   - ❑ a. calculate how much an employee was paid at another company.
   - ❑ b. buy tools and supplies for an employee.
   - ❑ c. calculate how much a company should pay an employee.

2. A job description is used to work out a _____ for the job.
   - ❑ a. midpoint salary
   - ❑ b. scale grade
   - ❑ c. salary range

3. A job or position with a high value would
   - ❑ a. pay less than the average job.
   - ❑ b. pay more than the average job.
   - ❑ c. pay the same as the average job.

4. The first figure in the cost-of-employee calculator is
   - ❑ a. the salary of the employee.
   - ❑ b. the benefits paid to an employee.
   - ❑ c. the tools and supplies used by the employee.

5. The midpoint, or mean, of a salary is
   - ❑ a. the average amount of two salaries.
   - ❑ b. the highest amount in a salary range.
   - ❑ c. the lowest amount in a salary range.

Understanding Ideas

6. The scale grade for a job is based on
   - ❑ a. how well a person does his or her job.
   - ❑ b. how important that job is to the success of the company.
   - ❑ c. how often a person comes in to work.

7. Paid vacations and paid sick days cost the company money because
   - ❑ a. the company is paying for work that is not being done.
   - ❑ b. the company has to train someone else to work while the employee is gone.
   - ❑ c. days off cost the company more money than work days.

8. The most important thing the HR department needs to know before deciding on a salary for a job is
   - ❑ a. the salary range.
   - ❑ b. the job description.
   - ❑ c. the cost of the employee to the company.

9. A cost-of-employee calculator is used by HR to
   - ❑ a. find out the scale value for the job.
   - ❑ b. find out how much a person should be paid at a job.
   - ❑ c. find out how much it costs the company to have a person work at a job.

10. One can conclude that HR departments
    - ❑ a. make sure that some people are paid more than others.
    - ❑ b. keep employees working hard.
    - ❑ c. keep costs from going too high.

Betting on the Best Health Plan

The cost of health care is very high. When a person needs to see a doctor or go into the hospital, health insurance will pay for most of these high costs.

Health insurance is a benefit that some businesses offer their employees. Often these businesses pay most of the monthly cost of each employee's health insurance. Insurance companies offer employees more than one plan to choose from. One plan may cost $323.86 a month and another may cost $215.40 a month. Why are the costs so different? One reason is that the deductible for the first plan is $1,000 and for the second it is $5,000. The deductible is the total amount a person must pay the health insurance company for medical costs each year before the insurance company begins to pay. Employees who choose an insurance plan with a $1,000 deductible pay more per month for the insurance than those who choose a $5,000 deductible. Those who choose the $5,000 deductible are hoping that their medical costs for that year, if any, will be low. This is because they have to pay any cost up to the limit of $5,000 if they are treated at a doctor's office or a hospital.

1. **Recognizing Words in Context**

   Find the word *benefit* in the passage. One definition below is closest to the meaning of that word. One definition has the opposite or nearly the opposite meaning. The remaining definition has a completely different meaning. Label the definitions C for *closest*, O for *opposite or nearly opposite*, and D for *different*.

   _____ a. support or aid

   _____ b. neglect

   _____ c. medicine

2. **Distinguishing Fact from Opinion**

   Two of the statements below present *facts*, which can be proved. The other statement is an *opinion*, which expresses someone's thoughts or beliefs. Label the statements F for *fact* and O for *opinion*.

   _____ a. People have to pay a deductible before insurance begins to pay for medical expenses.

   _____ b. Deductibles for health insurance are too high.

   _____ c. Insurance companies offer different plans for different needs.

3. Keeping Events in Order

Number the statements below 1, 2, and 3 to show the order in which the events take place.

_____ a. A person pays the insurance deductible.

_____ b. The insurance company pays the remaining costs of the medical bill.

_____ c. A person needs an expensive operation.

4. Making Correct Inferences

Two of the statements below are correct *inferences*, or reasonable guesses. They are based on information in the passage. The other statement is an incorrect, or faulty, inference. Label the statements C for *correct* inference and F for *faulty* inference.

_____ a. An employee does not pay the monthly insurance cost if he or she has no medical costs that year.

_____ b. Employees who see a doctor often every year would choose the lower deductible.

_____ c. An employee pays less of the monthly cost of health insurance than the business pays.

5. Understanding Main Ideas

One of the statements below expresses the main idea of the passage. One statement is too general, or too broad. The other explains only part of the passage; it is too narrow. Label the statements M for *main idea*, B for *too broad*, and N for *too narrow*.

_____ a. Employees who have a health insurance benefit can choose among one or more plans.

_____ b. Health insurance helps people with medical expenses.

_____ c. Some health plans offer a $5,000 deductible.

Correct Answers, Part A _____

Correct Answers, Part B _____

Total Correct Answers _____

Saving with Compound Interest

People save money for many reasons. Some people put their money in a savings account. Banks pay interest on the money that is in the account. The money in the savings account is called the principal. The interest that the bank pays the customer on the principal is expressed as a percentage. When people put money into a savings account, they usually try to find one with the highest interest rate.

Most savings accounts use compound interest. If it uses compound interest, the bank pays interest on the principal and also on the interest that the principal has earned up to that moment. The interest is added to the principal—it is compounded—and that new amount becomes the new principal that earns interest. That means that you make money not only on the money you first put in but also on the money you made. And this keeps happening over and over. The interest might be compounded once a year, every three months, once a month, once a week, or even every day.

A mathematical formula is used to calculate compound interest. The formula is based on the idea that the principal is multiplied by the interest rate to determine the interest. The formula changes depending on how often the deposit is compounded and on the number of years the deposit is in the bank. An example will make all this clearer.

Let's say a person puts $1,000 into a savings account that pays 3.5 percent interest. If the interest is compounded once a year, then at the end of the first year the principal will have earned an interest of $35. What if the interest is compounded quarterly, which is four times a year? After a year, that $1,000 would increase to $1,035.46. After two years, it would increase to $1,072.18. The first year the principal earned $35.46, which is more than 3.5 percent interest. It equals 3.546 percent interest based on the original principal. The second year it earned $36.72, which is 3.672 percent interest on the original principal. Because of compounding, the principal increases each year. At the end of 10 years, that $1,000 will have grown to $1,416.91.

But what if the interest had been compounded on a monthly or even a daily basis? With monthly compounding, the savings account would earn $35.57 the first year. With daily compounding, the principal would earn $35.62 the first year. Over time, a few cents can make a big difference.

Reading Time _____

Recalling Facts

1. The money in a savings account that gains interest is the
   - ❑ a. compound interest.
   - ❑ b. principal.
   - ❑ c. interest rate.

2. A mathematical formula used to calculate compound interest is based on the idea that
   - ❑ a. the principal is multiplied by the interest rate to determine the interest.
   - ❑ b. the interest is multiplied by the interest rate to determine the principal.
   - ❑ c. the interest rate is multiplied by the principal to determine the interest.

3. If a person puts $1,000 into an account that pays 3.5 percent interest, and the interest is compounded once a year, then at the end of the year the principal will have earned an interest of
   - ❑ a. $35,000.
   - ❑ b. $1,035.
   - ❑ c. $35.

4. Compound interest is interest earned on the principal
   - ❑ a. paid once every year.
   - ❑ b. and also on the interest that the principal has earned.
   - ❑ c. and doubles each time it is applied to the principal.

5. Interest that is compounded quarterly is paid to the principal
   - ❑ a. four times a year.
   - ❑ b. once a year.
   - ❑ c. once a month.

Understanding Ideas

6. One might infer from this passage that
   - ❑ a. the higher the amount of the principal, the higher the interest rate.
   - ❑ b. simple interest is better than compound interest.
   - ❑ c. the higher the amount of the principal, the more interest is earned.

7. Principal would grow faster with which compounded interest rate?
   - ❑ a. 3.5 percent
   - ❑ b. 3.0 percent
   - ❑ c. 4.0 percent

8. One can conclude that the principal grows faster
   - ❑ a. when interest is compounded once a year.
   - ❑ b. when interest is compounded quarterly.
   - ❑ c. when interest is compounded once a week.

9. With compound interest, the longer the principal stays in a savings account,
   - ❑ a. the faster your interest rate will change.
   - ❑ b. the more your principal will grow.
   - ❑ c. the higher the interest rate will grow.

10. What would *not* be a true statement from a bank offering compound interest?
    - ❑ a. "Your money is earning money for you."
    - ❑ b. "Your money is earning a little bit more month by month."
    - ❑ c. "Your $10 will grow to $100 in just one week."

The Rule of 72

A "rule of thumb" is a shortcut or a commonsense approach to a situation. The Rule of 72 is a financial rule of thumb. This rule helps you estimate how long it will take for you to double your money with compound interest. It's simple, but it's also pretty accurate.

The Rule of 72 is really just a division problem. The dividend is always 72. The divisor is the interest rate—but as a whole number, not a percentage. If the interest rate is 4 percent, you would just divide by 4. The quotient is the number of years it will take for the money to double.

Take an example in which you are investing $2,000 at 4 percent interest. If you divide 72 by 4, you will get 18. That's it. The Rule of 72 says at 4 percent interest it would take about 18 years to double your money. If you did the calculations using the formula for compound interest, your result would be more "on the money." On some day between the end of 17 years and the end of 18 years, you would get to $4,000. The Rule of 72 rounded that to 18 years, which is a good estimate.

1. **Recognizing Words in Context**

   Find the word *accurate* in the passage. One definition below is closest to the meaning of that word. One definition has the opposite or nearly the opposite meaning. The remaining definition has a completely different meaning. Label the definitions C for *closest*, O for *opposite or nearly opposite*, and D for *different*.

   _____ a. truthful

   _____ b. misleading

   _____ c. changed

2. **Distinguishing Fact from Opinion**

   Two of the statements below present *facts*, which can be proved. The other statement is an *opinion*, which expresses someone's thoughts or beliefs. Label the statements F for *fact* and O for *opinion*.

   _____ a. The Rule of 72 is better than using the formula for compound interest.

   _____ b. The Rule of 72 is a simple division problem.

   _____ c. The Rule of 72 provides an estimate of time needed to double money.

3. Keeping Events in Order

Number the statements below 1, 2, and 3 to show the order in which the steps should be performed.

_____ a. Divide 72 by the interest rate.

_____ b. Convert the interest rate to a whole number.

_____ c. Choose the interest rate.

4. Making Correct Inferences

Two of the statements below are correct *inferences,* or reasonable guesses. They are based on information in the passage. The other statement is an incorrect, or faulty, inference. Label the statements C for *correct* inference and F for *faulty* inference.

_____ a. The Rule of 72 is not useful if you plan to take your money out of the bank in a year.

_____ b. The Rule of 72 is useful only if you have a lot of money in the savings account.

_____ c. The Rule of 72 is useful only if your money is earning compound interest.

5. Understanding Main Ideas

One of the statements below expresses the main idea of the passage. One statement is too general, or too broad. The other explains only part of the passage; it is too narrow. Label the statements M for *main idea,* B for *too broad,* and N for *too narrow.*

_____ a. The Rule of 72 can be a commonsense approach to a situation.

_____ b. The Rule of 72 is a quick way to estimate how long it will take for you to double your money with compound interest.

_____ c. The Rule of 72 shows that it takes 18 years for money to double at 4 percent interest.

Correct Answers, Part A _____

Correct Answers, Part B _____

Total Correct Answers _____

Supply and Demand at the Window Factory

The production manager at Work Rite Windows must be sure that his customers are well served during the busy construction season. The factory has six weeks of orders to fill but also has a large number of windows in stock. The manager's knowledge of supply and demand and simple arithmetic will help him to figure out whether he has enough windows in stock to fill the orders. If not, he will have to build the rest of the windows he needs.

Supply, or inventory, is how much of a product is on hand. Demand is how much of a product customers want. The production manager must first figure out the current supply so he can decide how many windows his crew needs to build, based on the demand. The factory sells six different sizes of windows labeled A through F. He discovers that the factory has 2,200 total of types A, B, and C windows and 850 total of types D, E, and F windows.

Next, the manager calculates the demand by looking at the backlog of orders to fill. After adding up all the orders, he finds that the demand is a total of 2,700 of types A, B, and C windows and 1,420 of types D, E, and F. The manager must now subtract the supply from the demand so he knows how many windows of each size must still be made. He subtracts the 2,200 A, B, and C windows in inventory from the 2,700 he needs for orders. The difference is −500. This means his crew must build 500 of these types of windows. He then calculates how many of types D, E, and F need to be built by subtracting the supply of 850 from the demand of 1,420. The difference again is a negative number, −570. That means he needs a total of 1,070 windows to fill the present orders (500 + 570 = 1,070.)

The manager knows that his crew of 24 people can build 96 windows a day. However, four of his people will be on vacation for the next three weeks. He computes that each of his employees builds an average of four windows a day (96 ÷ 24 = 4). That means that when his crew is down to 20 people, they should average 80 windows per day (20 × 4 = 80). The manager then divides the number of additional windows needed by 80 and finds that his company will be able to fill all of the new orders after 13.375 working days.

Reading Time _____

Recalling Facts

1. Inventory is another word for _____, which is the amount of a product on hand.
   - ❑ a. demand
   - ❑ b. order
   - ❑ c. supply

2. How much of a product customers want is called
   - ❑ a. demand.
   - ❑ b. supply.
   - ❑ c. stock.

3. To find how many windows he needs, the manager
   - ❑ a. subtracts the supply from the demand.
   - ❑ b. divides the supply by the demand.
   - ❑ c. subtracts the demand from the supply.

4. After figuring the supply, the production manager needs to
   - ❑ a. measure the size of each window.
   - ❑ b. schedule the hours his crew needs to work.
   - ❑ c. determine how many windows are in demand.

5. The manager knows his 24 workers can build 96 windows a day, so to find how many windows one person can make, his calculation is
   - ❑ a. $96 - 24$.
   - ❑ b. 96×24.
   - ❑ c. $96 \div 24$.

Understanding Ideas

6. Why is it important for the manager to know that he has six weeks of orders for windows to fill?
   - ❑ a. In six weeks the demand might equal the supply.
   - ❑ b. He does not know how many workers will be taking a vacation.
   - ❑ c. If supply is less than demand, he will have to build more windows.

7. If a company has 630 windows in stock and orders for 720, the number of additional windows needed would be determined by
   - ❑ a. subtracting 630 from 720.
   - ❑ b. adding 720 and 630.
   - ❑ c. subtracting 90 from 630.

8. If the demand for 1,070 windows is reduced to 950 windows, what would the manager likely *not* do?
   - ❑ a. build the 1,070 windows and create a supply
   - ❑ b. stop work on the windows and create a demand
   - ❑ c. order his workers to build only 950 windows

9. If a company has 50 windows in inventory and orders for 30, it
   - ❑ a. has more demand than supply.
   - ❑ b. will have to build 20 windows.
   - ❑ c. has greater supply than demand.

10. Which of the following is *not* true?
    - ❑ a. It is better to have high demand and low supply than the other way around.
    - ❑ b. It is better to have low demand and high supply than the other way around.
    - ❑ c. It is better to have high demand and high supply than the other way around.

The Craftsman House

In the early 20th century, Gustav Stickley designed a style of house called "Craftsman." Stickley wanted to offer houses that were easy to pay for yet beautiful in design. Space, line, and angle, all familiar to you from your geometry studies, are used well in Craftsman houses. They are built with wide overhangs, deep porches, and narrowing pillars. They are mostly constructed of wood or stone. Inside, Craftsman houses call attention to form and function. Space is simply and creatively used for living, with design elements that make use of built-in spaces such as benches and cabinets.

Craftsman houses are easy to recognize. From the front, the straight roofline with several feet of overhang makes perfect 90-degree angles to the sides of the house. Triangular gables with windows often jut from the roof. Covered porches are often deep enough to be used as extra sitting areas. The outside design includes horizontal or vertical straight lines with few angles. This straight-line design makes the Craftsman house look clean and simple.

The inside of the Craftsman house also has the straight-line design. Square and rectangular entryways often have no doors, which adds to the feeling of open space. Wood moldings frame all doorways and windows.

1. **Recognizing Words in Context**

   Find the word *jut* in the passage. One definition below is closest to the meaning of that word. One definition has the opposite or nearly the opposite meaning. The remaining definition has a completely different meaning. Label the definitions C for *closest*, O for *opposite or nearly opposite*, and D for *different*.

   _____ a. stand

   _____ b. retreat

   _____ c. stick out

2. **Distinguishing Fact from Opinion**

   Two of the statements below present *facts*, which can be proved. The other statement is an *opinion*, which expresses someone's thoughts or beliefs. Label the statements F for *fact* and O for *opinion*.

   _____ a. Gustav Stickley wanted to make beautiful homes that people could afford to buy.

   _____ b. Craftsman houses use straight-line designs for a clean and simple look.

   _____ c. Everyone likes Craftsman-style houses.

3. Keeping Events in Order

Number the statements below 1, 2, and 3 to show the order in which the events took place.

_____ a. People began building and purchasing Craftsman houses.

_____ b. Gustav Stickley designed a new type of house called the Craftsman house.

_____ c. Gustav Stickley wanted to offer an affordable yet beautiful home.

4. Making Correct Inferences

Two of the statements below are correct *inferences,* or reasonable guesses. They are based on information in the passage. The other statement is an incorrect, or faulty, inference. Label the statements C for *correct* inference and F for *faulty* inference.

_____ a. Main rooms inside the house are open and have few doors.

_____ b. The clean lines and simple angles are meant to provide a feeling of hurry and excitement.

_____ c. Curves and rounded surfaces are used very little in Craftsman design.

5. Understanding Main Ideas

One of the statements below expresses the main idea of the passage. One statement is too general, or too broad. The other explains only part of the passage; it is too narrow. Label the statements M for *main idea,* B for *too broad,* and N for *too narrow.*

_____ a. Craftsman houses are designed simply and creatively.

_____ b. The Craftsman house has a simple design that appealed to home buyers in the early 20th century.

_____ c. Craftsman houses use open space and simple lines and angles in an attractive design.

Correct Answers, Part A _____

Correct Answers, Part B _____

Total Correct Answers _____

Olympic Scoring Systems

A scoring system is a mathematical procedure for expressing an athlete's performance in terms of a number of points to determine a winner in a sporting event. There are many different scoring systems. Some Olympic competitions are scored on the basis of ten points for first place, eight for second, and so on. In other competitions, scoring is five points for first place, three for second, two for third, and one for fourth. The team or competitor with the highest—or in some systems, the lowest—total score wins.

Gymnastics usually has four judges and one head judge. The four judges' scores are passed to the head judge, who removes the highest and lowest scores, averages the remaining scores, and divides the average by two. For example, if the judges vote 9.60, 9.80, 9.50, and 9.70, the head judge discards 9.80 and 9.50—the highest and lowest scores. The middle scores are averaged by adding them up and dividing by two. So 9.70 + 9.60 = 19.30, and 19.30 ÷ 2 = 9.65, which is the final score. Sometimes computers are used to calculate scores.

Synchronized swimming has a scoring system similar to the one used for figure skating. The competition is divided into a technical routine lasting up to three minutes and a free routine lasting up to five minutes. A panel of ten judges awards scores from 0 to 10 in one-tenth point increments. Usually, five judges look at the technical skill of the competitor, while the other five evaluate their artistic impression.

Both routines have requirements and are judged on level of difficulty, mistakes, creativity of movement, and performance. The technical routine counts for 35 percent of the total score and the free routine for 65 percent. The highest and lowest technical and artistic scores in each category are removed and the remaining scores averaged. The sum of scores in the technical merit category is multiplied by six. The sum of scores for artistic impression is multiplied by four. The total of these numbers equals the final routine score.

For the heptathlon, points are awarded for the best performance in each of seven events. The Greek word *hepta* means "seven" and *athlon* is a suffix meaning "contest." The heptathlon starts with the 100-meter hurdles, high jump, shot put, and 200-meter race on the first day. The long jump, javelin, and 800-meter race complete the competition on the following day. The athlete with the most points for all seven events wins.

Reading Time _____

Recalling Facts

1. A scoring system is
   - ❏ a. a computer program.
   - ❏ b. a way to calculate points.
   - ❏ c. an Olympic event.

2. A gymnastics head judge looks at the four other judges' scores and
   - ❏ a. adds the scores and divides the total by four.
   - ❏ b. discards the low and high scores.
   - ❏ c. multiplies the total score by two.

3. Which of the following is *not* true?
   - ❏ a. In some Olympic competitions the lowest total score wins.
   - ❏ b. The technical routine in synchronized swimming counts for 35 percent of the total score.
   - ❏ c. There are no requirements for the technical and artistic routines in figure skating.

4. Synchronized swimming and figure skating are judged similarly in that
   - ❏ a. each routine is judged on level of difficulty, mistakes, creativity of movement, and performance.
   - ❏ b. each judge looks at the technical skill of the competitor and at artistic impression.
   - ❏ c. the endurance of the performers is judged.

5. Points for the heptathlon are awarded for
   - ❏ a. technical skill and artistic impression.
   - ❏ b. energy and strength.
   - ❏ c. the best performance in each of the seven events.

Understanding Ideas

6. If you were a gymnastics head judge and the scores were 9.30, 9.40, 9.60, and 9.90, you would average
   - ❏ a. 9.40 and 9.60.
   - ❏ b. 9.30 and 9.40.
   - ❏ c. 9.30 and 9.90.

7. In the situation described in question 6, the final score you would turn in would be
   - ❏ a. 9.60.
   - ❏ b. 9.45.
   - ❏ c. 9.50.

8. It seems likely from this passage that synchronized swimmers
   - ❏ a. need to score highest in the free routine
   - ❏ b. can make more mistakes in the free routine than in the technical routine.
   - ❏ c. need to score highest in the technical routine.

9. One can infer that
   - ❏ a. athletes in the heptathlon are judged partly on artistic impression.
   - ❏ b. artistic impression is just as important as technique in synchronized swimming.
   - ❏ c. judges would find it hard to look at artistic impression and technical skill at the same time.

10. One can conclude from the information that
    - ❏ a. the athlete who places first always gets 10 points in the Olympics.
    - ❏ b. different Olympic events use different scoring systems.
    - ❏ c. the Olympic scoring system for gymnastics is the most difficult.

7 B Scoring in the Heptathlon

In 1984 the Olympic pentathlon, the women's athletics event, was replaced by the heptathlon. The heptathlon is a two-day contest. The first day includes the 100-meter hurdles, the high jump, the shot put, and the 200-meter dash. The second day includes the long jump, the javelin throw, and the 800-meter run.

Athletes in the heptathlon score points based on how well they do in each event. The athlete with the most total points at the end of the last event wins. The complex scoring system makes certain that an athlete who might dominate in one event cannot score as highly as someone who performs well in multiple events. The scoring for each event is set according to what is believed to be possible in that event, based on world records. A chart shows what an athlete's time or distance will be worth in points.

For example, in the 1988 Olympic Games, gold-medal winner Jackie Joyner-Kersee of the United States earned points for each of the seven events in the heptathlon. Points were given for her performances in the long jump (23 feet, 10¼ inches), the javelin throw (149 feet, 10 inches), the 800-meter race (2 minutes, 8 seconds), and so on. Her total of 7,291 points is still the world record.

1. **Recognizing Words in Context**

   Find the word *dominate* in the passage. One definition below is closest to the meaning of that word. One definition has the opposite or nearly the opposite meaning. The remaining definition has a completely different meaning. Label the definitions C for *closest*, O for *opposite or nearly opposite*, and D for *different*.

   _____ a. trail behind

   _____ b. be the strongest

   _____ c. uncover

2. **Distinguishing Fact from Opinion**

   Two of the statements below present *facts*, which can be proved. The other statement is an *opinion*, which expresses someone's thoughts or beliefs. Label the statements F for *fact* and O for *opinion*.

   _____ a. Joyner-Kersee set the world record with a score of 7,291 points in the heptathlon.

   _____ b. Joyner-Kersee competed in seven events in the heptathlon.

   _____ c. Joyner-Kersee is the best female athlete of all time.

3. **Keeping Events in Order**

Number the statements below 1, 2, and 3 to show the order in which the events took place.

_____ a. The heptathlon replaced the pentathlon in the Olympics.

_____ b. Joyner-Kersee won a gold medal at the Seoul Olympics.

_____ c. The pentathlon was a women's combined athletics event.

4. **Making Correct Inferences**

Two of the statements below are correct *inferences,* or reasonable guesses. They are based on information in the passage. The other statement is an incorrect, or faulty, inference. Label the statements C for *correct* inference and F for *faulty* inference.

_____ a. Joyner-Kersee is best known as an athlete who dominated the heptathlon.

_____ b. Anyone who can win the heptathlon can break a world record.

_____ c. Joyner-Kersee is a role model for young athletes.

5. **Understanding Main Ideas**

One of the statements below expresses the main idea of the passage. One statement is too general, or too broad. The other explains only part of the passage; it is too narrow. Label the statements M for *main idea,* B for *too broad,* and N for *too narrow.*

_____ a. The javelin throw is part of the heptathlon.

_____ b. Joyner-Kersee has won many awards.

_____ c. The heptathlon is a competition that requires many skills.

Correct Answers, Part A _____

Correct Answers, Part B _____

Total Correct Answers _____

　　　　Lewis Carroll's Games

Lewis Carroll is best known as the author of *Alice's Adventures in Wonderland* and *Through the Looking-Glass*. However, he was also a skilled mathematician, logician, and photographer. He was interested in games, and he enjoyed creating many different types of word and number puzzles. These puzzles require patience and logical thinking in addition to math skills. The next paragraph is one of Lewis Carroll's most familiar puzzles. As you read, think about how you might solve it.

A queen and her son and daughter were locked in a room at the top of a lofty tower. Outside their window was a pulley with a rope through it. Both ends of the rope reached the ground, and identical baskets were tied to them. The queen and her children used the rope-and-pulley apparatus to escape to safety, aided by a 75-pound stone found in the tower room. They knew that as one basket was lowered, the other would rise. Safe lowering could occur only if the difference in the weight of the baskets and their contents was no more than 15 pounds. The queen weighed 195 pounds, the daughter weighed 105 pounds, and the son weighed 90 pounds. How did they all escape?

In order to solve the puzzle, think about the relationships among the weights of the three people as well as the stone they found in the room. Consider the fact that the weight of the baskets must not differ more than 15 pounds. Think of options based on addition and subtraction. Can you solve the puzzle? The next paragraph gives the solution.

First the son sent the stone down and the empty basket came up. He then proceeded down as the stone came up. The daughter took the stone out, and then she traveled down as the son came back up. The son got out of the basket, sent the stone down, and the empty basket came back up. The queen then proceeded down as the daughter and stone came back up. The daughter got out, sent the stone back down, and the empty basket came back up. The son traveled down, and the stone came up. The daughter removed the stone and proceeded down as the son came back up. The son got out, sent the stone down, and the empty basket came up. The son traveled down, and the stone came up. He got out, and the basket and stone fell to the ground.

Reading Time _____

Recalling Facts

1. Lewis Carroll is best known as
   - ❏ a. a mathematician.
   - ❏ b. an author.
   - ❏ c. a logician.

2. The queen and her children
   - ❏ a. lived in a castle.
   - ❏ b. climbed to the top of the tower.
   - ❏ c. were locked in a room atop a tower.

3. The son was the first to get in the basket because
   - ❏ a. he was braver than his mother or sister.
   - ❏ b. he weighed more than his mother or sister.
   - ❏ c. his weight was within 15 pounds of the weight of the stone.

4. The stone found in the tower weighed
   - ❏ a. 75 pounds.
   - ❏ b. 90 pounds.
   - ❏ c. 15 pounds.

5. The only person who did not go back up to the top during the escape was
   - ❏ a. the queen.
   - ❏ b. the son.
   - ❏ c. the daughter.

Understanding Ideas

6. One might infer from this passage that
   - ❏ a. the queen and her children could not have escaped without the aid of the stone.
   - ❏ b. the daughter was older than the son.
   - ❏ c. the fact that the son's weight was less than his mother's helped them to escape.

7. To solve the puzzle, the number 15 was important because there was a difference of 15 pounds in the weights of
   - ❏ a. the daughter and the basket.
   - ❏ b. the son and the queen.
   - ❏ c. the son and the daughter.

8. If the weight in the two baskets varied more than 15 pounds,
   - ❏ a. the lighter basket would have fallen rapidly to the ground.
   - ❏ b. both baskets would have stayed at the top.
   - ❏ c. the heavier basket would have fallen rapidly to the ground.

9. Finding the solution to this puzzle involved
   - ❏ a. subtraction.
   - ❏ b. addition and subtraction.
   - ❏ c. addition.

10. One can conclude that finding answers to number puzzles
    - ❏ a. is always done very quickly.
    - ❏ b. often depends on logic and math skills.
    - ❏ c. depends on luck.

Mathematical Puzzles

Since the time of the ancient Egyptians, people have been challenging one another with mathematical puzzles. Some old puzzles still have not been solved. Searching for answers to puzzles has led to the advancement of various forms of math. Many mathematical puzzles pose a question that can be answered using a simple math application. The following puzzle is an example.

A swimming pool has three pipes for adding water. The gray pipe fills the pool in two hours. The gold pipe fills the pool in three hours, while the brown pipe fills it in four hours. The drain pipe empties the pool in 12 hours. How long will it take to fill the pool if all pipes are in operation?

Think about the rate at which each pipe fills the pool. Write the rates as fractions: ½, ⅓, ¼. Then use a common denominator: $\frac{6}{12}$, $\frac{4}{12}$, $\frac{3}{12}$. Now think of the drain as doing "negative work," because it is "unfilling" the pool. Its rate of work is $-\frac{1}{12}$. Then use the equation, "One (full pool) = rate × time." The answer to the puzzle is one hour $[1 = (\frac{6}{12} + \frac{4}{12} + \frac{3}{12} - \frac{1}{12}) \times 1]$.

1. Recognizing Words in Context

Find the word *advancement* in the passage. One definition below is closest to the meaning of that word. One definition has the opposite or nearly the opposite meaning. The remaining definition has a completely different meaning. Label the definitions C for *closest*, O for *opposite or nearly opposite*, and D for *different*.

_____ a. science

_____ b. progress

_____ c. retreat

2. Distinguishing Fact from Opinion

Two of the statements below present *facts*, which can be proved. The other statement is an *opinion*, which expresses someone's thoughts or beliefs. Label the statements F for *fact* and O for *opinion*.

_____ a. Solving mathematical puzzles has led to the discovery of various forms of math.

_____ b. People have been solving mathematical puzzles for many centuries.

_____ c. Mathematical puzzles are more fun than ordinary riddles.

3. Keeping Events in Order

Number the statements below 1, 2, and 3 to show the order in which steps should be performed.

_____ a. Determine the hourly rate at which each pipe fills the pool.

_____ b. Write the hourly rates as fractions and then use a common denominator.

_____ c. Find the rate of work that is done by the drain.

4. Making Correct Inferences

Two of the statements below are correct *inferences,* or reasonable guesses. They are based on information in the passage. The other statement is an incorrect, or faulty, inference. Label the statements C for *correct* inference and F for *faulty* inference.

_____ a. The pool is filled by all four pipes.

_____ b. The drain pipe is the slowest of the four pipes.

_____ c. Thinking of the drain as doing "negative work" is a way of stating the drain is not filling the pool.

5. Understanding Main Ideas

One of the statements below expresses the main idea of the passage. One statement is too general, or too broad. The other explains only part of the passage; it is too narrow. Label the statements M for *main idea,* B for *too broad,* and N for *too narrow.*

_____ a. Three pipes together will fill $^{13}\!/_{2}$ of the pool in one hour.

_____ b. Mathematical puzzles can be solved using simple equations.

_____ c. Mathematical puzzles may use words and numbers to pose a riddle.

Correct Answers, Part A _____

Correct Answers, Part B _____

Total Correct Answers _____

Comparing Temperatures in Different Climates

The climates of San Juan, Puerto Rico, and Bismarck, North Dakota, offer stark contrasts in temperature. When figuring in the heat index and wind chill factor, the contrast between these cities is even greater.

San Juan's climate is hot most of the year and changes little. The normal high in July is 88 degrees Fahrenheit, and the normal low is 76 degrees. That's a difference of 12 degrees during July ($88 - 76 = 12$). January's normal high is 83 degrees Fahrenheit, and the low is 70 degrees. That's a difference of 13 degrees during January ($83 - 70 = 13$). The difference between the July highs and January lows is only 18 degrees ($88 - 70 = 18$).

When the heat index is used, San Juan feels hotter. The heat index is a measure of how hot the combination of heat and humidity makes a person feel. The heat index uses mathematics to adjust warm temperatures according to the percentage of humidity in the air. High humidity is uncomfortable; the body cools off more slowly because sweat takes longer to dry. During July in San Juan, a high of 88 degrees with humidity of 67 percent feels like 99 degrees. That's 11 degrees higher than the actual air temperature.

Bismarck's climate is colder than San Juan's, and the temperature difference is much greater. The normal high in July is 84 degrees. That's close to San Juan's high of 88 degrees. The normal July low in Bismarck, though, is 56 degrees. That's a difference of 28 degrees during the month ($84 - 56 = 28$). Recall that San Juan's difference is only 12 degrees. The biggest contrast between the cities is in winter. January's normal high in Bismarck is 19 degrees, and the low is a frosty −1 degree. That's 64 and 71 degrees colder than San Juan for the month.

When wind chill factors are used, Bismarck feels colder. Wind chill is a measure of how cold the combination of temperature and wind makes a person feel. The wind chill uses mathematics to adjust cold temperatures according to wind speed. The greater the wind speed, the faster a person will lose body heat. On a winter day in Bismarck, a high of 19 degrees with a wind of 9.5 miles per hour makes it feel like 8 degrees. That's 11 degrees colder than the air temperature. In contrast, San Juan's winter high with the heat index is 83 degrees, or 75 degrees warmer.

Reading Time _____

Recalling Facts

1. The average July high temperature in Bismarck is
   - ❏ a. much lower than the average July high temperature in San Juan.
   - ❏ b. about the same as the average July high temperature in San Juan.
   - ❏ c. much higher than the average July high temperature in San Juan.

2. Temperatures in San Juan
   - ❏ a. change most during the winter.
   - ❏ b. change a lot year round.
   - ❏ c. change very little year round.

3. The July temperature range in Bismarck is
   - ❏ a. 28 degrees.
   - ❏ b. about the same as in San Juan.
   - ❏ c. 20 degrees.

4. The heat index adjusts warm temperatures according to the percentage of
   - ❏ a. heat in the air.
   - ❏ b. wind speed.
   - ❏ c. humidity in the air.

5. The wind chill is a measure of the combination of
   - ❏ a. cold temperature and body heat.
   - ❏ b. cold temperature and humidity.
   - ❏ c. cold temperature and wind speed.

Understanding Ideas

6. You can conclude from the information in this article that
   - ❏ a. wind chill is more important in Bismarck than in San Juan.
   - ❏ b. wind chill is more important in San Juan than in Bismarck.
   - ❏ c. heat index is more important in Bismarck than in San Juan.

7. The greater the wind speed, the faster a person will lose
   - ❏ a. body heat.
   - ❏ b. humidity.
   - ❏ c. sweat.

8. The wind chill factor can make the temperature feel about
   - ❏ a. 10 degrees colder.
   - ❏ b. 25 degrees warmer.
   - ❏ c. 10 degrees warmer.

9. The heat index can make the temperature feel about
   - ❏ a. 10 degrees colder.
   - ❏ b. 25 degrees colder.
   - ❏ c. 10 degrees warmer.

10. Bismarck's temperature difference is much greater than San Juan's, which means
    - ❏ a. the air temperature is much hotter in San Juan than in Bismarck.
    - ❏ b. the difference in summer and winter temperatures is greater in Bismarck than it is in San Juan.
    - ❏ c. the air temperature is much colder in Bismarck than in San Juan.

How to Read a Natural Gas Bill

Most people read only the amount due on their monthly natural gas heating bill. If your bill is excessive, you might want to know the mathematics behind the bill. You will need to look at the charges for gas used and heat supplied.

A gas bill is based on the amount of gas used by the customer. A gas meter at your home measures the amount used in units of 100 cubic feet (CCF). If your present reading is 1,422 CCF this month and it was 1,248 CCF last month, the difference is 174 CCF.

The gas company converts the amount of gas used to a measure of the heat that was supplied. The CCF amount is multiplied by the Btu factor. One Btu is the amount of heat needed to raise the temperature of one pound of water by one degree Fahrenheit. It's more or less the heat produced by one lit match. The Btu factor is used to compute therms. One therm is equal to 100,000 Btus. Your bill might show that 174 (CCF) × 1.023 (therms conversion factor) equals 178.0 therms.

The bill shows the cost of therms. The cost of one therm might be $0.25, so 178 × $0.25 = $44.50. That is the payment that is due.

1. **Recognizing Words in Context**

   Find the word *excessive* in the passage. One definition below is closest to the meaning of that word. One definition has the opposite or nearly the opposite meaning. The remaining definition has a completely different meaning. Label the definitions C for *closest,* O for *opposite or nearly opposite,* and D for *different.*

   _____ a. too much

   _____ b. reasonable

   _____ c. up-to-date

2. **Distinguishing Fact from Opinion**

   Two of the statements below present *facts,* which can be proved. The other statement is an *opinion,* which expresses someone's thoughts or beliefs. Label the statements F for *fact* and O for *opinion.*

   _____ a. A gas bill is based on the amount of gas used by the customer.

   _____ b. The Btu factor is used to compute therms.

   _____ c. Gas companies charge too much for heat.

3. **Keeping Events in Order**

Number the statements below 1, 2, and 3 to show the order in which the events would take place.

_____ a. The number of therms used is calculated.

_____ b. The amount of gas used (CCF) is calculated.

_____ c. The cost of therms is calculated.

4. **Making Correct Inferences**

Two of the statements below are correct *inferences,* or reasonable guesses. They are based on information in the passage. The other statement is an incorrect, or faulty, inference. Label the statements C for *correct* inference and F for *faulty* inference.

_____ a. Reducing the amount of gas used can lower gas bills.

_____ b. Gas bills do not show how much gas was used in a month.

_____ c. Most people trust that the amount they are charged for gas is correct.

5. **Understanding Main Ideas**

One of the statements below expresses the main idea of the passage. One statement is too general, or too broad. The other explains only part of the passage; it is too narrow. Label the statements M for *main idea,* B for *too broad,* and N for *too narrow.*

_____ a. A gas bill shows the amount the gas company charges for gas.

_____ b. A gas bill is based on the amount of gas used by the customer.

_____ c. A gas bill shows charges for the amount of gas used and heat supplied.

Correct Answers, Part A _____

Correct Answers, Part B _____

Total Correct Answers _____

What Is Geometry?

Geometry is the pure mathematics of points and lines and curves and surfaces. The word *geometry* means "measurement of the earth." Many jobs, from measuring a wall area for painting to conducting scientific research, use principles of geometry. The following example shows one common use of geometry.

The yard around Tim's new home is all mud. He decides to lay rolls of sod, which is like a carpet of ready-grown grass. To figure out how much sod to purchase, Tim measures his whole yard and uses some simple geometry. He knows that one roll of sod covers 12 square feet. His backyard is 50 feet wide and 20 feet long, or 1,000 square feet in area. His front yard is 50 feet wide and 12 feet long, or 600 square feet in area. So his total area is 1,600 square feet. He divides that by the square footage of each roll of sod and finds that he needs 134 rolls of sod.

Ancient people used geometry to map their land, to help them plan roads and buildings, and to better understand the objects in the spaces around them. Around 300 B.C.E. Euclid became the first person to organize the principles of geometry. One principle of Euclidean geometry is that a straight line is the shortest distance between two points. From this and other ideas, the Greeks formed new ideas about points, lines, angles, curves, and planes. With only a ruler and a compass, the Greeks measured the area of two-dimensional figures such as circles, squares, and triangles. They also measured the volume of solids, or three-dimensional figures, such as cubes and cones.

The next great move forward was analytic geometry, which was introduced by René Descartes in 1637. He showed how relations between points in a plane can be expressed algebraically. Analytic geometry is important in math history because it connected algebra (number relationships) and geometry (space relationships).

Another type of geometry is descriptive geometry. This has to do with making two-dimensional drawings of three-dimensional objects. Still other types have moved beyond three dimensions. Non-Euclidean geometry, for example, deals with space. Euclid believed that two parallel lines would never meet no matter how far they stretched. This principle, long held to be true, is no longer accepted in modern ideas about the universe. Einstein's famous theory of relativity is based on non-Euclidean geometry.

Reading Time _____

Recalling Facts

1. All geometry involves
   - ❏ a. two-dimensional shapes.
   - ❏ b. scientific research.
   - ❏ c. measuring and describing spaces.

2. Tim found the area of his yard by
   - ❏ a. multiplying its width by its depth.
   - ❏ b. adding its width and depth.
   - ❏ c. dividing its width by its depth.

3. Euclid was the first person to
   - ❏ a. measure the area of two-dimensional figures.
   - ❏ b. measure the volume of solids.
   - ❏ c. organize the principles of geometry.

4. Analytic geometry links
   - ❏ a. trigonometry and geometry.
   - ❏ b. algebra and geometry.
   - ❏ c. basic and descriptive geometry.

5. Descriptive geometry involves
   - ❏ a. moving beyond three dimensions.
   - ❏ b. making two-dimensional drawings of three-dimensional objects.
   - ❏ c. making three-dimensional drawings of two-dimensional objects.

Understanding Ideas

6. Which of the following might best describe ways ancient people used geometry?
   - ❏ a. They could work out problems with unknown factors.
   - ❏ b. They could measure area and objects.
   - ❏ c. They could count in multiples.

7. René Descartes's contribution to advanced geometry was that he
   - ❏ a. invented algebraic analysis.
   - ❏ b. was the first to connect number relationships and space relationships.
   - ❏ c. formed new ideas about points, lines, angles, curves, and planes.

8. One could infer that non-Euclidean geometry
   - ❏ a. was the belief that two parallel lines would never meet no matter how far they stretched.
   - ❏ b. deals with dimensions beyond the third dimension.
   - ❏ c. was introduced by Einstein in his theory of relativity.

9. The example of Tim measuring his yard shows an application of measuring
   - ❏ a. the area of two-dimensional figures.
   - ❏ b. the volume of a three-dimensional figure.
   - ❏ c. the shortest distance between two points.

10. The kind of geometry that measures two-dimensional figures such as circles, squares, and triangles is called
    - ❏ a. Euclidean geometry.
    - ❏ b. analytic geometry.
    - ❏ c. nonlinear geometry.

10 | B | Pauline Sperry

Even with improved test scores, girls still fall behind boys in math achievement. Today's girls may find a hero in Pauline Sperry. She stood out in the field of mathematics long before most women began to work outside of the home.

Sperry was born in Massachusetts in 1885. She studied and taught math at Smith College. In 1912 she began graduate work in geometry at the University of Chicago. She earned a master's degree in mathematics in 1914, and two years later she earned a Ph.D. In 1917 Sperry became a teacher at the University of California at Berkeley, where she worked for more than 30 years. She became the first female assistant professor in the math department in 1923. She later became an associate professor.

Sperry's skill was geometry, and she taught many of these courses at the school. She taught honors students as well as students studying for their final degrees. Sperry also wrote two books on geometry.

In 1950 Sperry and 30 other teachers were fired when they refused to sign a political statement they did not believe in. In 1952 a court ruling gave them back their jobs. After she retired, Sperry worked for political causes until her death in 1967.

1. **Recognizing Words in Context**

   Find the word *achievement* in the passage. One definition below is closest to the meaning of that word. One definition has the opposite or nearly the opposite meaning. The remaining definition has a completely different meaning. Label the definitions C for *closest*, O for *opposite or nearly opposite*, and D for *different*.

   _____ a. success

   _____ b. failure

   _____ c. command

2. **Distinguishing Fact from Opinion**

   Two of the statements below present *facts*, which can be proved. The other statement is an *opinion*, which expresses someone's thoughts or beliefs. Label the statements F for *fact* and O for *opinion*.

   _____ a. Sperry was the best teacher in the math department.

   _____ b. Sperry was the first female assistant professor in her department.

   _____ c. Sperry wrote two books on geometry.

3. Keeping Events in Order

Number the statements below 1, 2, and 3 to show the order in which the events took place.

_____ a. Sperry refused to sign a political statement.

_____ b. Sperry worked for political causes.

_____ c. In 1912 Sperry began graduate work in geometry at the University of Chicago.

4. Making Correct Inferences

Two of the statements below are correct *inferences,* or reasonable guesses. They are based on information in the passage. The other statement is an incorrect, or faulty, inference. Label the statements C for *correct* inference and F for *faulty* inference.

_____ a. She was a good teacher, but Sperry wanted to do more than teach.

_____ b. She worked hard to get the best job she could in mathematics.

_____ c. Sperry did not want girls to look up to her as a role model.

5. Understanding Main Ideas

One of the statements below expresses the main idea of the passage. One statement is too general, or too broad. The other explains only part of the passage; it is too narrow. Label the statements M for *main idea,* B for *too broad,* and N for *too narrow.*

_____ a. Pauline Sperry taught geometry for 30 years and wrote two books on the subject.

_____ b. Pauline Sperry was a pioneer among female mathematicians.

_____ c. Pauline Sperry was the first female assistant mathematics professor at the University of California at Berkeley.

Correct Answers, Part A _____

Correct Answers, Part B _____

Total Correct Answers _____

Pick a card, any card! What are the chances you will draw a particular card? To answer that question, you need to understand probability. Probability is the study of all possible outcomes of events ruled by the chances of getting each of these outcomes. The probability of an outcome is expressed as a number between zero and one. The closer the probability is to zero, the less likely it is that the outcome will happen. The closer the probability is to one, the more likely it is that the outcome will happen.

A deck of playing cards can help you learn to calculate probability. If you choose one card, what is the probability it will be red? You can find the answer using three steps. First, you must find the number of all favored outcomes. A 52-card deck holds 13 red diamonds and 13 red hearts. So there are 26 possible *favored* outcomes. Next, you must find the total number of *possible* outcomes. If you select any card from the deck, there are 52 possible outcomes. To determine the probability, you divide the number of favored outcomes by the number of possible outcomes. The 26 favored outcomes divided by 52 possible outcomes equals 0.5. So the probability of selecting a red card is .5, or 50 percent.

What is the probability of selecting a club? A standard deck contains 13 clubs. You divide 13 favored outcomes by 52 possible outcomes and get 0.25. The probability of selecting a club is .25, or 25 percent.

What is the probability of selecting the ace of spades out of all the spades? The favored outcome is just one, the ace of spades. Instead of 52 possible outcomes, however, there are now just 13, the total number of spades in the deck. When you divide 1 by 13, the probability of drawing the ace of spades is 0.077, or a little less than 10 percent.

Probability can be used for card tricks, and it also can be used in business. Insurance companies base their entire business on probability. Life insurance companies use statistical studies to predict the probability that people will live to a certain age. Home insurance companies use probability to predict damage from storms or fires. In business, probability isn't as easy to calculate as drawing from a deck of 52 cards. Many people are living longer than expected, and nobody knows when an act of nature will cause damage. So every time a death or a flood does or does not occur, insurance companies update the expected probability of the next occurrence.

Reading Time _____

Recalling Facts

1. Probability is the study of all possible outcomes of events
   - ❏ a. ruled by any number of possible favored outcomes.
   - ❏ b. ruled by the probability of getting any of these outcomes.
   - ❏ c. ruled by the chances of getting each of these outcomes.

2. Probability is expressed as a number
   - ❏ a. between one and two.
   - ❏ b. between zero and one.
   - ❏ c. between 26 and 52.

3. The higher the probability,
   - ❏ a. the lower the chance an event will occur.
   - ❏ b. the greater the chance an event will occur.
   - ❏ c. the more often a chance will occur.

4. When determining the probability of choosing the right card, the first step is to
   - ❏ a. find the total number of possible outcomes.
   - ❏ b. find the total number of chances.
   - ❏ c. find the total number of favored outcomes.

5. _____ use probability in their business to predict probability that people will live to a certain age.
   - ❏ a. Life insurance companies
   - ❏ b. Fire insurance companies
   - ❏ c. Car insurance companies

Understanding Ideas

6. To find the probability of selecting one of 13 clubs from a deck of 52 cards,
   - ❏ a. multiply the 13 favored outcomes by the 52 possible outcomes.
   - ❏ b. divide the 13 favored outcomes by the 52 possible outcomes.
   - ❏ c. divide the 52 possible outcomes by the 13 favored outcomes.

7. The probability of selecting a diamond is _____ the probability of selecting a heart.
   - ❏ a. greater than
   - ❏ b. the same as
   - ❏ c. less than

8. How is the probability of choosing an ace calculated?
   - ❏ a. $1 \div 52$
   - ❏ b. $4 \div 13$
   - ❏ c. $4 \div 52$

9. For insurance companies, the number of possible outcomes is
   - ❏ a. the chance that an event will happen.
   - ❏ b. the number of times an event has occurred in the past.
   - ❏ c. the same as the chance that an event will not happen.

10. Which of the following statements is *not* true about probability?
    - ❏ a. Probability is easier to calculate if the number of possible occurrences is unknown.
    - ❏ b. For insurance companies, a possible occurrence is something that has happened before.
    - ❏ c. Probability is a way for businesses to guess what will happen.

The Positive and Negative Numbers Game

Games can make learning more interesting. One particular game uses a deck of playing cards to practice adding and subtracting positive and negative numbers. Here's how the game is played.

The game can have two or more players. The dealer deals an equal number of cards to the players, and the leftover cards are disregarded. The black cards represent positive numbers, and the red cards represent negative numbers. Jacks have a value of 11, queens a value of 12, and kings a value of 13. Aces have a value of one. Each player places his or her cards face down in a pile.

The player to the left of the dealer begins the game by turning one card face up and calling out its number. For example, a four of hearts would be "negative four." The next player turns over a card. That player places his or her card on top of the first card and calculates the sum of the two. If the card is black, the value is added. If the card is red, the value is deducted. Then the player says the total aloud. The next player repeats this process. The game ends when the total is exactly 25.

1. **Recognizing Words in Context**

   Find the word *disregarded* in the passage. One definition below is closest to the meaning of that word. One definition has the opposite or nearly the opposite meaning. The remaining definition has a completely different meaning. Label the definitions C for *closest*, O for *opposite or nearly opposite*, and D for *different*.

   _____ a. piled up

   _____ b. included

   _____ c. put aside

2. **Distinguishing Fact from Opinion**

   Two of the statements below present *facts*, which can be proved. The other statement is an *opinion*, which expresses someone's thoughts or beliefs. Label the statements F for *fact* and O for *opinion*.

   _____ a. The game ends when the sum of the cards equals 25.

   _____ b. The king of diamonds has a value of negative 13.

   _____ c. This game is more fun when played very fast.

3. Keeping Events in Order

Number the statements below 1, 2, and 3 to show the order in which the events take place.

_____ a. The player to the left of the dealer turns up one card, saying the number aloud.

_____ b. A player adds a card that brings the stack's total to 25.

_____ c. The dealer deals an equal number of cards to each player.

4. Making Correct Inferences

Two of the statements below are correct *inferences,* or reasonable guesses. They are based on information in the passage. The other statement is an incorrect, or faulty, inference. Label the statements C for *correct* inference and F for *faulty* inference.

_____ a. A steady drawing of red cards could send the sums into negative numbers.

_____ b. The ace is the least valuable card because it equals one.

_____ c. Totals that go above 25 would require red cards to bring the total down.

5. Understanding Main Ideas

One of the statements below expresses the main idea of the passage. One statement is too general, or too broad. The other explains only part of the passage; it is too narrow. Label the statements M for *main idea,* B for *too broad,* and N for *too narrow.*

_____ a. This math game ends when the total is exactly 25.

_____ b. Playing a game is a fun way to teach mathematics.

_____ c. Students can practice adding positive and negative numbers by playing a card game.

Correct Answers, Part A _____

Correct Answers, Part B _____

Total Correct Answers _____

Symmetry means "balance of form." Something that is symmetrical has equal proportions. You can see examples of symmetry all around you in nature, art, and architecture. It is used in floor plans of buildings and in designing doors, windows, floors, and more.

A picture or some other form that is not in balance is *asymmetrical.* Artists use both symmetry and asymmetry in their work. Some use symmetry to create order and harmony. Others use asymmetry because they feel that life is out of balance or unfair. They use their art to reflect this feeling. Both symmetry and asymmetry play important roles in shaping the beauty of an object.

M.C. Escher was an artist who enjoyed using symmetry in his prints and drawings. He liked to show the order that weaves through our rich and complicated world.

There are many variations of symmetry, but the three most common are reflectional, translational, and rotational. The most familiar type of symmetry is reflectional, or "mirror," symmetry. A butterfly and the letter T are examples of reflectional symmetry. If you imagine a line going down the center of an object, one side is a mirror image of the other side. The letters "db" are an example of mirror symmetry.

The second type, translational symmetry, represents movement of a design in a linear direction. If you copy a design and put that copy right next to the original, you are moving the design in a linear direction. An example of translation symmetry is "Hello-Hello."

The third common type of symmetry is rotational symmetry. An image has rotational symmetry if it looks the same when rotated, or turned, a certain number of times around a center point. For example, a triangle, if turned around three times, will look the same all three times. A four-leaf clover will match itself four times as it is turned around a center point.

Cubism was an art movement that broke up the geometry of space and form. The Cubists created asymmetrical art to express the imperfection of human life. They created their own reality by showing things out of balance and painting pieces of objects. Instead of viewing subjects from one angle, the Cubists broke the images up so that different angles of the subject could be seen at the same time. Cubism had a major impact on artists during the first decades of the 20th century, and it remains one of the most famous art forms today.

Reading Time _____

Recalling Facts

1. Something that is asymmetrical is
   - ❑ a. not in balance.
   - ❑ b. a mirror image.
   - ❑ c. unfair.

2. Symmetry means
   - ❑ a. not even.
   - ❑ b. balance of form.
   - ❑ c. nature, art, and architecture.

3. An example of reflectional symmetry would be
   - ❑ a. a butterfly.
   - ❑ b. a banana.
   - ❑ c. the letter P.

4. An image has rotational symmetry if
   - ❑ a. the design moves in a linear direction.
   - ❑ b. both sides look the same when the image is held up to a mirror.
   - ❑ c. it looks the same when turned around a center point.

5. The artist M.C. Escher used symmetry in his work to show
   - ❑ a. pieces of objects.
   - ❑ b. the order in the world.
   - ❑ c. many sides at the same time.

Understanding Ideas

6. One can infer from the information in this passage that the human body has
   - ❑ a. rotational symmetry.
   - ❑ b. translational symmetry.
   - ❑ c. reflectional symmetry.

7. The geometric form of a circle has
   - ❑ a. rotational symmetry.
   - ❑ b. both reflectional symmetry and rotational symmetry.
   - ❑ c. translational symmetry.

8. From the ideas in the article, you could infer that translational symmetry would likely be used in
   - ❑ a. designing masks.
   - ❑ b. designing playing cards.
   - ❑ c. designing wallpaper.

9. You could infer from this article that a Cubist painting
   - ❑ a. would be symmetrical.
   - ❑ b. would show the subject from different angles.
   - ❑ c. would look realistic.

10. You could conclude from this article that
   - ❑ a. there are only three variations of symmetry.
   - ❑ b. symmetry and asymmetry are important in shaping the beauty of an object.
   - ❑ c. art that is asymmetrical does not reflect real life.

Pablo Picasso was born in 1881 and began studying art in 1892. During his long life as an artist, he created paintings, sculptures, drawings, pottery, and engravings.

In 1907 Picasso and Georges Braque met in Paris. They worked together until 1914, starting the Cubist movement. Their goal was to express nature in simple, geometric forms. The idea was to show everyday things as the mind, not the eye, saw them—from all sides at once. To this end in their art, they took natural shapes apart and put them together again with intersecting planes.

The Young Ladies of Avignon is often called the first Cubist picture. Picasso finished it in 1907. The women seem to be joined to the background, making the picture space look flat. Picasso completed *The Head of a Young Woman* in 1913. This painting shows parts of an eye, a chin, and a shoulder in an arrangement of rectangles and circles.

Later on the Cubists experimented with different materials. Instead of painting images, they pasted real materials such as bus tickets or menus onto the canvas in a technique called collage.

After Picasso's death in 1973, thousands of his pieces went to the Picasso Museum in Paris.

1. **Recognizing Words in Context**

   Find the word *intersecting* in the passage. One definition below is closest to the meaning of that word. One definition has the opposite or nearly the opposite meaning. The remaining definition has a completely different meaning. Label the definitions C for *closest*, O for *opposite or nearly opposite*, and D for *different*.

   _____ a. simple

   _____ b. crossing

   _____ c. parallel

2. **Distinguishing Fact from Opinion**

   Two of the statements below present *facts*, which can be proved. The other statement is an *opinion*, which expresses someone's thoughts or beliefs. Label the statements F for *fact* and O for *opinion*.

   _____ a. Cubists experimented with pasting real materials onto canvas.

   _____ b. Sometimes the picture space in a Cubist painting looks flat.

   _____ c. Cubist art is disturbing to look at.

3. Keeping Events in Order

Number the statements below 1, 2, and 3 to show the order in which the events took place.

_____ a. Picasso completed *The Young Ladies of Avignon.*

_____ b. Picasso met Braque in Paris.

_____ c. Picasso completed *The Head of a Young Woman.*

4. Making Correct Inferences

Two of the statements below are correct *inferences,* or reasonable guesses. They are based on information in the passage. The other statement is an incorrect, or faulty, inference. Label the statements C for *correct* inference and F for *faulty* inference.

_____ a. Picasso and Braque wanted their art to reflect the world as they saw it.

_____ b. Picasso painted *The Head of a Young Woman* with rectangles and circles because he wanted to show her as ugly.

_____ c. The Cubist artists believed their art showed real life.

5. Understanding Main Ideas

One of the statements below expresses the main idea of the passage. One statement is too general, or too broad. The other explains only part of the passage; it is too narrow. Label the statements M for *main idea,* B for *too broad,* and N for *too narrow.*

_____ a. Picasso's art helped define the Cubist movement.

_____ b. Picasso and the Cubists showed natural objects in simple, geometric forms.

_____ c. Picasso and the Cubists expressed themselves through their art.

Correct Answers, Part A _____

Correct Answers, Part B _____

Total Correct Answers _____

Are people better off today than they were 10 or 100 years ago? Are they healthier? Questions like these can be answered by studying the information provided by statistics. Statistics is a branch of mathematics. It uses numbers as a way to look at the world we live in. One way to measure whether people are better off today is to see whether they are living longer. Life expectancy is the average number of years people born in a given year are expected to live. People who study life expectancy look for patterns in the statistics concerning people's lives—their health, wealth, family size, and other factors. They study the data and calculate how long, given these and other factors, people can expect to live.

Healthy People 2010, a U.S. government program, provides these statistics on life expectancy. At the beginning of the 20th century, a child born in the United States was expected to live an average of 47.3 years. That average today is about 77 years. Since 1929 the average has increased by about 20 years. In the last 10 years, life expectancy has increased by 1.5 years. On average, life expectancy in the United States is higher for females than it is for males. In 2002, for example, the average life expectancy of females was 79.9 years, compared with 74.5 years for males.

Note that a person's life expectancy depends on the year he or she was born, not on what year it is now. People today who are 65 years old can expect to live an average of 18 more years. Those aged 75 years can expect to live an average of 11 more years.

Average life expectancy of people around the world has increased in the last few hundred years. According to the *World Population Data Sheet,* in 2004 the average life expectancy was 67 years (65 years for males and 69 years for females). There are major differences in life expectancy in some regions. For example, in 2004 Africa's people had an average life expectancy of 52 years. In Europe the average was 74 years. In Asia life expectancy was 67 years.

At least 18 countries with populations of one million or more have life expectancies greater than the United States. People who study statistics look at many factors as possible reasons why. One important factor is lifestyle choices that affect health. Smoking and eating habits and exercise all have an effect on life expectancy for certain age groups.

Reading Time _____

Recalling Facts

1. Life expectancy is
   - ❏ a. the average number of years a person born in a given year is expected to live.
   - ❏ b. the average number of years a healthy person is expected to live.
   - ❏ c. the average age to which a person is expected to live.

2. At the beginning of the 20th century, a child born in the United States was expected to live an average of
   - ❏ a. 65 years.
   - ❏ b. 46.5 years.
   - ❏ c. 47.3 years.

3. In 2002 the average life expectancy in the United States was about
   - ❏ a. 79.9 years.
   - ❏ b. 77 years.
   - ❏ c. 74.5 years.

4. In 2004 the average life expectancy was 67 years, which was the same as the average for
   - ❏ a. Asia.
   - ❏ b. Africa.
   - ❏ c. Europe.

5. At least _____ countries with populations of one million or more have life expectancies greater than the United States.
   - ❏ a. 11
   - ❏ b. 18
   - ❏ c. 65

Understanding Ideas

6. Based on the information in the passage, the average U.S. life expectancy was
   - ❏ a. greater than the world average.
   - ❏ b. less than the world average.
   - ❏ c. the same as the world average.

7. The increased U.S. life expectancy over the last 100 years probably is due to
   - ❏ a. better medicine and health care.
   - ❏ b. the invention of television and the computer.
   - ❏ c. cleaner air and water.

8. A factor that probably does *not* contribute much to changes in life expectancy is
   - ❏ a. the number of rest days.
   - ❏ b. availability of well-paying jobs.
   - ❏ c. the number of warm and cold days.

9. One can conclude that
   - ❏ a. life expectancies for people over 75 are longer now.
   - ❏ b. life expectancies in 100 years will be double what they are now.
   - ❏ c. life expectancies increased by 10 percent every year since 1900.

10. Which statement best sums up the passage?
    - ❏ a. Life expectancy has increased on average all over the world.
    - ❏ b. Life expectancy is a measure of how much better off people are today than 100 years ago.
    - ❏ c. Life expectancy is calculated by studying statistics related to the life style of people.

13 | B | Social Security and Life Expectancy

Over the last 60 years, life expectancy has risen. Because Americans are living longer, Social Security benefits are being paid for longer periods. The success of Social Security depends on having enough people working and paying into the program.

Social Security is a government program that supports workers who are retired. People can begin receiving funds when they turn 62. The amount received depends on how much a person has earned during his or her working life. Social Security is paid for by workers and businesses through taxes. In 2004 workers will pay 7.65 percent of their earnings up to $87,900. This means the most that workers will pay in that year is $87,900 × 0.0765, or $6,724.35. The accumulated money collected from workers is kept in a fund that pays the benefits to retired people.

An uncommonly large group of people called "baby boomers," born between 1946 and 1964, entered the work force between the mid-1960s and the mid-1980s. Their earnings are helping to support retired workers. It's a matter of simple mathematics. The Social Security fund is expected to grow until about 2012, when most of the baby boomers will retire. After that, the number of workers paying into Social Security will be smaller. So the amount in the fund will be smaller also.

1. Recognizing Words in Context

Find the word *accumulated* in the passage. One definition below is closest to the meaning of that word. One definition has the opposite or nearly the opposite meaning. The remaining definition has a completely different meaning. Label the definitions C for *closest*, O for *opposite or nearly opposite*, and D for *different*.

_____ a. taken away

_____ b. built up

_____ c. paid

2. Distinguishing Fact from Opinion

Two of the statements below present *facts*, which can be proved. The other statement is an *opinion*, which expresses someone's thoughts or beliefs. Label the statements F for *fact* and O for *opinion*.

_____ a. The success of Social Security depends on having enough people paying into the program.

_____ b. Social Security benefits are the best way of funding people's retirement.

_____ c. Social Security is funded by workers and businesses through taxes.

63

3. Keeping Events in Order

Number the statements below 1, 2, and 3 to show the order in which the events take place.

_____ a. Retired workers receive Social Security payments.

_____ b. Workers pay into Social Security through taxes.

_____ c. Social Security taxes paid by workers build up in a fund.

4. Making Correct Inferences

Two of the statements below are correct *inferences,* or reasonable guesses. They are based on information in the passage. The other statement is an incorrect, or faulty, inference. Label the statements C for *correct* inference and F for *faulty* inference.

_____ a. A person who continues to work after age 62 no longer needs to pay into the Social Security fund.

_____ b. The more money earned by people currently working, the more benefits will be available to retired persons.

_____ c. Social Security fund benefits are affected by the number of people working and the amount they are paid.

5. Understanding Main Ideas

One of the statements below expresses the main idea of the passage. One statement is too general, or too broad. The other explains only part of the passage; it is too narrow. Label the statements M for *main idea,* B for *too broad,* and N for *too narrow.*

_____ a. Life expectancy plays a major role in how well the Social Security system can help retired people.

_____ b. Social Security is based on a percentage of workers' earnings.

_____ c. Social Security benefits are paid to people when they retire after the age of 62.

Correct Answers, Part A _____

Correct Answers, Part B _____

Total Correct Answers _____

Rhythm Patterns in Thai Classical Music

Two types of traditional music have developed throughout Thailand's history: folk and classical. People in the Thai countryside played and enjoyed folk music. Classical music was limited to the royal court. In 1932 when Thailand was no longer governed by a single ruler, classical music became available to everyone.

Thai classical music interests people who listen to music and who study music. Part of its appeal is in the way the rhythms of the notes are layered. Many different rhythm patterns are played by several pitched and nonpitched percussion instruments at the same time. A bell is an example of a pitched percussion instrument. Most drums are nonpitched.

A measure is a small section of musical time that arranges musical notes into beats. Western music often has four beats in a measure, with a quarter note equaling one beat. Most Thai classical music is in duple meter, in which each measure of music has two beats. In both Western and Thai music, a quarter note usually equals one beat. Both often subdivide each beat into smaller parts. An eighth note receives half a beat and a sixteenth note receives a quarter of a beat.

A typical measure might have a pattern of two sixteenth notes followed by an eighth note and a quarter note. Added together, these notes equal two full beats. A second measure could include a pattern of one eighth note, two sixteenth notes, and two eighth notes. Again, these notes add up to two full beats. A third two-beat measure could include a pattern of six sixteenth notes and one eighth note.

Rhythm patterns that echo each other can be played. A drum might play a pattern of one eighth note, two sixteenth notes, and one quarter note. A second instrument could play one quarter note followed by one eighth note and two sixteenth notes. The rhythm pattern of the second beat in the second rhythm pattern is exactly the same as the first beat of the first rhythm pattern. When played at the same time over and over, the two instruments will sound like they are chasing each other.

Thai classical music uses a variety of two-beat measures, such as those described above, and repeats patterns over and over. The patterns will or will not be pitched, depending on the instruments. The sound of multiple rhythmic patterns played at the same time creates beautiful layers of rhythm and pitch.

Reading Time _____

Recalling Facts

1. Until 1932, the only people who could listen to Thai classical music were
   - ❏ a. Thai people who lived in the countryside.
   - ❏ b. visitors to Thailand.
   - ❏ c. the royal court of Thailand.

2. A bell is an example of a
   - ❏ a. drum.
   - ❏ b. pitched percussion instrument.
   - ❏ c. nonpitched percussion instrument.

3. Most Thai classical music is written in
   - ❏ a. triple meter.
   - ❏ b. duple meter.
   - ❏ c. uneven meters.

4. A small section of musical time that arranges the musical notes into beats is called
   - ❏ a. a duple meter.
   - ❏ b. a measure.
   - ❏ c. a rhythm.

5. A measure in duple meter has
   - ❏ a. notes that equal one full beat.
   - ❏ b. notes that equal four quarter notes.
   - ❏ c. notes that equal two full beats.

Understanding Ideas

6. You can infer from the information in this passage that
   - ❏ a. much of Thai classical music uses percussion instruments.
   - ❏ b. modern Thai pop music is written only in duple meter.
   - ❏ c. Thai classical music is often sung.

7. If one beat in duple meter is made with two eighth notes, then the second beat can be made with
   - ❏ a. six sixteenth notes.
   - ❏ b. one quarter note.
   - ❏ c. one eighth note and one quarter note.

8. If a measure of music written in duple meter begins with two sixteenth notes followed by two eighth notes, the measure could end with
   - ❏ a. one quarter note.
   - ❏ b. two sixteenth notes.
   - ❏ c. two eighth notes.

9. You could infer from this article that someone studying how beats work in Thai music would be most interested in
   - ❏ a. its use of pitched percussion instruments.
   - ❏ b. its royal history.
   - ❏ c. its multiple rhythm patterns played at the same time.

10. You can conclude from the information in this passage that Thai classical music
    - ❏ a. includes beautifully written melody lines.
    - ❏ b. is the basis for pop music in Thailand today.
    - ❏ c. is best known for using multiple rhythm patterns.

14 B The Geometry of the Chula Kite

Kites are made in many geometric shapes, such as triangles, rectangles, and the always-popular quadrangle. One popular kite in Thailand is the Chula. This kite uses many geometrical shapes within shapes.

First of all, the Chula's five-pointed star shape lends it a certain resemblance to a human being. The framework is made of nine pieces of bamboo. Three of the bamboo sections are straight and six are curved. The top or head of the kite is triangular. The arms and legs are symmetrical, or identical on each side.

The Chula's arms use one large shape similar to an oval but with pointed ends. Both legs connect to a single straight line of bamboo. Then each leg stretches into two arches, forming a fin shape that connects at the bottom. The framework is tied tightly together using square, crisscross patterns of threads. Then thin paper is glued to the front of the bamboo frame.

The Chula kite is used in the popular Thai sport of kite fighting. Teams use their skills to try to take down their opponents' kites. Nonfighting Thai kites come in many shapes and sizes. Probably no other Thai kite is as geometrically complex as the five-pointed Chula kite.

1. Recognizing Words in Context

Find the word *resemblance* in the passage. One definition below is closest to the meaning of that word. One definition has the opposite or nearly the opposite meaning. The remaining definition has a completely different meaning. Label the definitions C for *closest*, O for *opposite or nearly opposite*, and D for *different*.

_____ a. likeness

_____ b. attraction

_____ c. difference

2. Distinguishing Fact from Opinion

Two of the statements below present *facts*, which can be proved. The other statement is an *opinion*, which expresses someone's thoughts or beliefs. Label the statements F for *fact* and O for *opinion*.

_____ a. Kite fighting is more fun than simply flying a kite.

_____ b. The Chula kite has the shape of a human being.

_____ c. Many different geometric shapes are present in the body of a Chula kite.

3. Keeping Events in Order

Number the statements below 1, 2, and 3 to show the order in which the steps take place.

_____ a. Thin paper is glued to the front of the bamboo frame.

_____ b. The bamboo pieces are tied tightly together using square, crisscross patterns of threads.

_____ c. Nine bamboo pieces are cut to size.

4. Making Correct Inferences

Two of the statements below are correct *inferences,* or reasonable guesses. They are based on information in the passage. The other statement is an incorrect, or faulty, inference. Label the statements C for *correct* inference and F for *faulty* inference.

_____ a. The kite's square, crisscross patterns of threads give the kite strength necessary for fighting.

_____ b. The pointed arms of the Chula kite are helpful in a kite fight.

_____ c. All Thai fighter kites are shaped like the Chula kite.

5. Understanding Main Ideas

One of the statements below expresses the main idea of the passage. One statement is too general, or too broad. The other explains only part of the passage; it is too narrow. Label the statements M for *main idea,* B for *too broad,* and N for *too narrow.*

_____ a. Many kites are made in geometric shapes.

_____ b. The Chula kite uses many different geometric shapes.

_____ c. The frame of a Chula kite is made of nine pieces of bamboo.

Correct Answers, Part A _____

Correct Answers, Part B _____

Total Correct Answers _____

Worldwide Oil Reserves: Produce More or Conserve?

Many experts believe that in the next 15 years, world oil production will reach its all-time peak. Then the resources will run out. When production of oil begins to decline, the price of gasoline will skyrocket. Should we try to extract more oil, or just use less? The answer to this question will likely be debated for a long time. But it is helpful first to express the information mathematically.

The U.S. Energy Information Administration reports that in 2002, world oil and gas reserves equaled 1,032 Gbo. A Gbo stands for one billion barrels of oil. To figure out how long this amount will last, we must look at how much oil is used worldwide each year. In 2004 the world used about 28 Gbo of oil, with about 7.6 Gbo used by the United States alone. If we divide the 1,032 Gbo in reserve by 28, it would appear that in 2002 we had about 37 years' worth of oil remaining.

This number is misleading, however. First, we are using more oil each year. Worldwide usage has grown about 2 percent per year over the last few years. Some experts predict that by 2020, worldwide usage may rise to 40 Gbo, or 43 percent over present levels ($40 - 28 = 12$; $12 \div 28 = .43$). Second, there's no way of knowing exactly how much oil is left in the earth. Some experts think the reported oil reserves may be overestimated.

One way to slow down the usage of the earth's oil is to conserve, or use less. In the 1970s, American car makers made cars that could go farther on less fuel than they could before. If such fuel efficiency continues, the amount of oil used would go down. Over the next few years, better fuel economy is expected for some trucks. A 22.2 percent improvement in fuel economy is expected for aircraft. The less oil we use, the longer our reserves will last.

Experts disagree over whether oil conservation in the United States can affect worldwide supplies. Some believe that getting better fuel economy from auto makers can make a difference. Others think the best way to conserve our oil is not to waste it. When oil is used as fuel, it produces carbon dioxide that harms the air. The more oil we use, the more pollutants we produce. If we decrease the amount of energy we use to heat our homes by 20 percent, we would pay less for the heat, and the air would be less polluted.

Reading Time _____

Recalling Facts

1. Some experts predict that worldwide oil production may hit its peak
   - ❏ a. within the next 3 years.
   - ❏ b. within the next 15 years.
   - ❏ c. within the next 75 years.

2. When the production of oil begins to decline, the price of gasoline will
   - ❏ a. stay the same.
   - ❏ b. greatly increase.
   - ❏ c. slightly fall.

3. Gbo means
   - ❏ a. gallons of burning oil.
   - ❏ b. one million barrels of oil.
   - ❏ c. one billion barrels of oil.

4. In 2002 the world had oil and gas reserves of
   - ❏ a. 132 billion gallons.
   - ❏ b. 32 Gbo.
   - ❏ c. 1,032 Gbo.

5. In 2004 alone, the number of gallons of oil used in the United States was about
   - ❏ a. 43 Gbo.
   - ❏ b. 7.6 Gbo.
   - ❏ c. 110 Gbo.

Understanding Ideas

6. You can conclude from the information in this passage that
   - ❏ a. no one is certain how much oil remains to be used.
   - ❏ b. we won't need to worry about the earth's oil reserves for at least the next 100 years.
   - ❏ c. we have more than 37 years of worldwide oil reserves.

7. It would seem that U.S. truck and aircraft makers want to
   - ❏ a. use less oil.
   - ❏ b. use more oil.
   - ❏ c. sell fewer trucks.

8. Some experts think that improving fuel economy in heating our homes will help to
   - ❏ a. increase the cost of oil.
   - ❏ b. reduce oil conservation.
   - ❏ c. slow down the use of oil.

9. You can conclude from this passage that using less oil in the United States will
   - ❏ a. increase the amount of oil used in other countries.
   - ❏ b. help to reduce the earth's pollution.
   - ❏ c. reduce the amount of oil used in other countries.

10. The author of the passage might agree that
    - ❏ a. finding more efficient ways of using oil will slow down the depletion of the earth's supply.
    - ❏ b. we have large supplies of oil that are yet to be discovered.
    - ❏ c. we should not be concerned about the worldwide increase in oil usage.

The Energy Crisis of the 1970s

In 1973 an oil crisis caused panic across the United States. Gas prices rose from $0.30 per gallon to over $1.00 per gallon. Scenes of long lines at neighborhood gas stations fed the panic. Many people believed there was a worldwide oil shortage. The reason for the widespread panic is revealed through mathematics.

Oil use was high in the early 1970s, but U.S. oil production was declining. In just three years, the use of foreign oil in the United States rose from 22 to 36 percent. Most of the foreign oil was produced in the Middle East. Because of fighting in this region, Middle Eastern countries cut off oil sales to the United States. In a few months, the cost of foreign oil rose from about $3 to $12 per barrel. One barrel of crude oil equals 42 gallons. This amount of crude oil produces about 20 gallons of gasoline. It is easy to see how a large jump in foreign oil prices would drive up the cost of consumer gasoline. The "crisis" (at least in the short term) turned out not to be a real shortage but rather the result of oil producers holding back oil.

1. **Recognizing Words in Context**

   Find the word *declining* in the passage. One definition below is closest to the meaning of that word. One definition has the opposite or nearly the opposite meaning. The remaining definition has a completely different meaning. Label the definitions C for *closest*, O for *opposite or nearly opposite*, and D for *different*.

   _____ a. getting larger

   _____ b. getting cheaper

   _____ c. getting smaller

2. **Distinguishing Fact from Opinion**

   Two of the statements below present *facts*, which can be proved. The other statement is an *opinion*, which expresses someone's thoughts or beliefs. Label the statements F for *fact* and O for *opinion*.

   _____ a. People should not have believed there was a worldwide oil shortage.

   _____ b. In 1973, the cost of foreign oil increased by almost 75 percent.

   _____ c. A Middle Eastern oil stoppage helped cause the energy crisis.

3. Keeping Events in Order

Number the statements below 1, 2, and 3 to show the order in which the events took place.

_____ a. The use of foreign oil in the United States rose from 22 to 36 percent.

_____ b. Gas prices rose from $.30 per gallon to over $1.00 per gallon.

_____ c. Some Middle Eastern countries cut off exports of oil to America.

4. Making Correct Inferences

Two of the statements below are correct *inferences*, or reasonable guesses. They are based on information in the passage. The other statement is an incorrect, or faulty, inference. Label the statements C for *correct* inference and F for *faulty* inference.

_____ a. The 1973 oil crisis was made worse by people thinking there was less oil to be produced than there was.

_____ b. The cost of crude oil determines the price that people pay for gas.

_____ c. Americans were more careful about conserving oil after the energy crisis of the 1970s.

5. Understanding Main Ideas

One of the statements below expresses the main idea of the passage. One statement is too general, or too broad. The other explains only part of the passage; it is too narrow. Label the statements M for *main idea,* B for *too broad,* and N for *too narrow.*

_____ a. The 1970s energy crisis centered on the issues of oil.

_____ b. In 1973 many people believed the world oil supply was low.

_____ c. In 1973 scenes of long lines at neighborhood gas stations brought on a panic.

Correct Answers, Part A _____

Correct Answers, Part B _____

Total Correct Answers _____

ANSWER KEY

READING RATE GRAPH

COMPREHENSION SCORE GRAPH

COMPREHENSION SKILLS PROFILE GRAPH

ANSWER KEY

1A 1. b   2. b   3. c   4. c   5. b   6. b   7. a   8. b   9. c   10. c

1B 1. D, C, O   2. F, F, O   3. 2, 3, 1   4. C, C, F   5. N, M, B

2A 1. b   2. c   3. b   4. c   5. b   6. b   7. a   8. a   9. c   10. a

2B 1. D, C, O   2. F, O, F   3. 1, 2, 3   4. C, C, F   5. B, N, M

3A 1. c   2. b   3. c   4. c   5. a   6. a   7. a   8. c   9. b   10. a

3B 1. C, O, D   2. F, F, O   3. 3, 2, 1   4. C, F, C   5. B, N, M

4A 1. c   2. b   3. b   4. a   5. a   6. b   7. a   8. b   9. c   10. c

4B 1. C, O, D   2. F, O, F   3. 2, 3, 1   4. F, C, C   5. M, B, N

5A 1. b   2. a   3. c   4. b   5. a   6. c   7. c   8. c   9. b   10. c

5B 1. C, O, D   2. O, F, F   3. 3, 2, 1   4. C, F, C   5. B, M, N

6A 1. c   2. a   3. a   4. c   5. c   6. c   7. a   8. b   9. c   10. b

6B 1. D, O, C   2. F, F, O   3. 3, 2, 1   4. C, F, C   5. N, B, M

7A 1. b   2. b   3. c   4. a   5. c   6. a   7. c   8. a   9. c   10. b

7B 1. O, C, D   2. F, F, O   3. 2, 3, 1   4. C, F, C   5. N, B, M

8A 1. b   2. c   3. c   4. a   5. a   6. a   7. c   8. c   9. b   10. b

8B 1. D, C, O   2. F, F, O   3. 1, 2, 3   4. F, C, C   5. N, M, B

9A	1. b	2. c	3. a	4. c	5. c	6. a	7. a	8. a	9. c	10. b
9B	1. C, O, D		2. F, F, O		3. 2, 1, 3		4. C, F, C		5. B, N, M	
10A	1. c	2. a	3. c	4. b	5. b	6. b	7. b	8. b	9. a	10. a
10B	1. C, O, D		2. O, F, F		3. 2, 3, 1		4. C, C, F		5. B, M, N	
11A	1. c	2. b	3. b	4. c	5. a	6. b	7. b	8. c	9. b	10. a
11B	1. D, O, C		2. F, F, O		3. 2, 3, 1		4. C, C, F		5. N, B, M	
12A	1. a	2. b	3. a	4. c	5. b	6. c	7. b	8. c	9. b	10. b
12B	1. D, C, O		2. F, F, O		3. 2, 1, 3		4. C, F, C		5. N, M, B	
13A	1. a	2. c	3. b	4. a	5. b	6. a	7. a	8. c	9. a	10. c
13B	1. O, C, D		2. F, O, F		3. 3, 1, 2		4. F, C, C		5. N, M, B	
14A	1. c	2. b	3. b	4. b	5. c	6. a	7. b	8. b	9. c	10. c
14B	1. C, D, O		2. O, F, F		3. 3, 2, 1		4. C, C, F		5. B, M, N	
15A	1. b	2. b	3. c	4. c	5. b	6. a	7. a	8. c	9. b	10. a
15B	1. O, D, C		2. O, F, F		3. 1, 3, 2		4. C, C, F		5. B, M, N	

READING RATE

Put an X on the line above each lesson number to show your reading time and words-per-minute rate for that lesson.

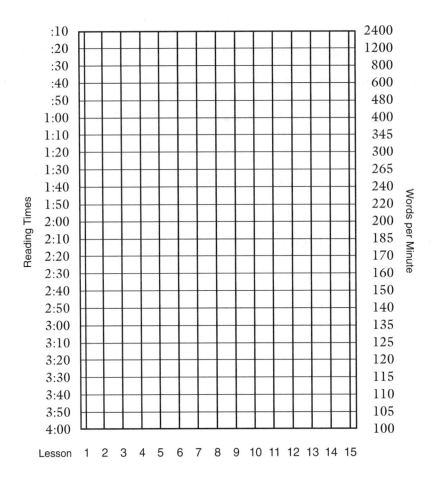

COMPREHENSION SCORE

Put an X on the line above each lesson number to indicate your total correct answers and comprehension score for that lesson.

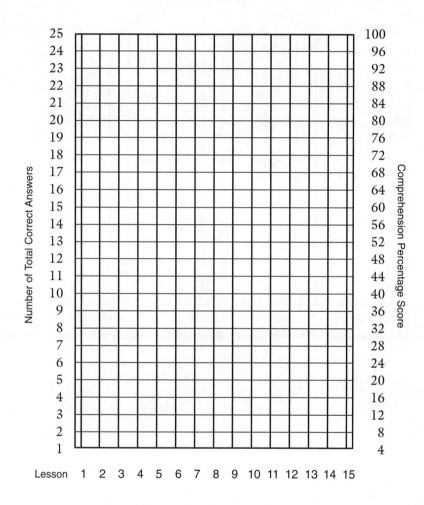

COMPREHENSION SKILLS PROFILE

Put an X in the box above each question type to indicate an incorrect response to any part of that question.

	Recognizing Words in Context	Distinguishing Fact from Opinion	Keeping Events in Order	Making Correct Inferences	Understanding Main Ideas
Lesson 1					
2					
3					
4					
5					
6					
7					
8					
9					
10					
11					
12					
13					
14					
15					